A River Remains

A River Remains

Poems by Larry Smith

WordTech Editions

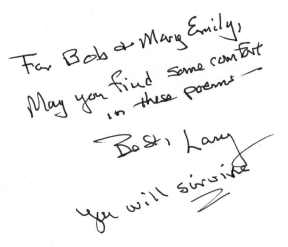

For Bob & Mary Emily,
May you find some comfort
in these poems —

Best, Larry
you will survive

Published by WordTech Editions
P.O. Box 541106
Cincinnati, OH 45254-1106

Typeset in Aldine by WordTech Communications LLC, Cincinnati, OH

ISBN: 1933456280
LCCN: 2006927688

Poetry Editor: Kevin Walzer
Business Editor: Lori Jareo

Visit us on the web at www.wordtechweb.com

Acknowledgments

The following poems were first published in these publications for which we give thanks.

Individual Poems:
"Working It Out" in *Tradeswomen Magazine* Sept./Oct. 1995. "Somewhere, Someone" *Coffeehouse Poetry Anthology*, Spring 1996. "The Visit" in *Prayers to Protest: Poems that Center and Bless Us.* Pudding House Publication, Fall 1997. "The Gathering" in *The Journal,* Spring 1997. "The Writing," *Rattle,* Winter 1998. "Ohio October, Route 4," in *Whetstone* 15, Spring 1998. "Ohio October, Route 4," "In the Middle of Rye Beach Road," "Polishing a Stone," in *Grand Lakes Review* 1998. "Taking Leave at Daybreak," *Red Brick Review* 1999. "Dreaming of Home," "Driving Back Home in Late Winter," and "Visiting My Sister in Southeast Ohio in a Snowstorm" in *RiverWind #27,* 2004. "Letter to d.a. levy in Existential Heaven," on deepcleveland junkmail oracle, 2003, and in *Heartlands Vol. 2,* 2004. "In Muddy Waters" in *Whiskey Island Magazine, #47,* 2004. "Rock and Rolling at the Hop," in *three chord poems: the poetry of rock and roll* in deepcleveland press 2005. "Last Words" in *Heartlands* Vol. 3, 2005. A portion of "Where You Are" is reprinted from *Turning Wheel: Buddhist Peace Fellowship,* winter 2006.

Collections:
"In Muddy Waters," "Following the Road," "Calligraphy of Birds" "Walking a Field into Evening," and "Into Still Air" in *America Zen: A Gathering of Poets,* Bottom Dog Press, 2004. "Two Tanka," "In Muddy Waters," "The Change," "Non-Sequitor Advantage," "Letter to d.a. levy in Existential Heaven" "Calligraphy of Birds," and "Reunion at Cross Creek" appeared in a chapbook collection #4 from green panda press, Summer 2004.

The poems of *After T'ang* and *Tanka and Haiku: Cut and Stacked* appeared in limited edition chapbooks from Harmony Books. "Shadows on the Water," "What You Realize When Cancer Comes," "Telling an Old Friend," "The Lighting," "The Visit," "Getting Word," and "The Bridge to Steubenville," appeared in *Milldust and Roses: Memoirs,* Ridgeway Press 2002.

Special thanks to fellow poets Diane Gilliam Fisher, Joel Rudinger, and to the Firelands Writing Center members for editing advice and to WordTech Communications for their dedication.

For Ann and for family and friends

Contents

One: After
Returning...17
Visiting My Sister in Southeast Ohio in a Snowstorm 18
Climbing the Knob Through the Trees in Early Spring.........19
Standing at the Lookout at Sheldon's Marsh.....................20
Driving Back Home in Late Winter 21
Walking at Old Woman's Creek with a Friend....................22
At Home in a Time of War 23
Lake Country in Early Morning...24
Winter Snow at Sunrise..25
By the River at Dusk..26
Walking a Field into Evening..27
Visiting My Sister Alone in Winter....................................28
Spring Solstice in the Woods at Dave and Guilda's............29
Looking Out onto My Back Porch in the Middle of Winter.....31
The Call..32
Early Rising...33
Walking the Neighborhood into Night...............................34
Visiting a Friend Along the Lake.......................................35
Rite of Passage at Sheldon's Marsh...................................36
Mount Tremper Before Dawn 37
Late Afternoon in Early Spring...38

Two: Cut and Stacked, Tanka and Haiku
Heart Beat Tanka 41
Bellingham Walk January #2..42
Walking Walden Pond 43
Sheldon's Marsh Preserve 45
Walking Tanka...46
Driving West..47
Mingo Tanka..48
After Yoga 49
Tanka Dog...50
Shoreline...51
Tanka Sequence After the Poet Saigyo...............................52
Haiku for Jack..55

Bellingham Walk January #1 56
Driving Down Ohio Route 13 57
Walking Haiku 58
Subway Haiku.. 61
At Home Haiku 63
Random Haiku 65
Into Still Air 66

Three: Native Grounds, What Is Near
Ohio Valley Vision 69
Our House on Murdock Street.. 70
What Is Near... 72
Along the Ohio 73
Business as Usual—Ohio Valley.. 74
Filling in the Background 75
Rock and Rolling in the 1950's.. 76
Working the Steam Table with Darlene 78
Working It Out.. 81
Where I Am Going/Where I Have Been.. 83
Driving Toward Home 84
Reunion at Cross Creek... 85
Mingo Junction—December 2002.. 86
Dreaming of Home 88
To the Silence of Men... 90
The Bridge to Steubenville 91

Four: Standing in Muddy Waters
Entering the Pain in Muddy Waters.. 95
A Father's Pain.. 96
Making My Hospice Visits... 97
The Alchemy of Pain... 99
The V.A. Medical Center... 102
Fading with the Night.. 104
Breakfast of Poets on Detroit Avenue... 105
Reaching Out/Holding On... 107
Letter to d.a. levy in Existential Heaven...................................... 108
Entering the Pain 110
The Alcohol Recovery House 112
Sickness 113
This Day.. 114

Writing in the Middle of the Night......................................115
Last Words...117
Touching It..118

Five: The Cancer Poems, Living with It
Reading the Skies..121
Shadows on the Water...123
What You Realize When Cancer Comes.......................................125
The Second Opinion...127
The Bone Scan..130
Resting..133
Visiting the Cleveland Museum of Natural History.........................134
Telling an Old Friend..136
The Lightning..138
The Massage..139
In the Fish Tank...140
Walking Through..141
The Testing in Seattle...143
The Writing..147
Thinking of You in Seattle...148
Working Around It..149
Gathering..151
This Is a Poem About...155
Recovering...156
Living with It...157
Recognition..158
Before the Sun...159
Leaning Together in a Storm..160
Man to Man...162
What Is Needed...164
The Turnings...165
Cancer Check-Up..168
Cancer Note..169

Six: Traveling, Taking Leave at Daybreak
Calligraphy of Birds...173
Canoeing in Mid-October..174
Sheldon's Marsh in Mid-Summer: "A Bird's Wing
    Sweeps the Sky"..176
Walking the Castalia Quarries..177

Taking Leave at Daybreak 178
Gliding 179
Magee Marsh in Early Spring 180
Sheldon's Marsh 181
Ohio October, Route 4 182
Polishing a Stone 183
In the Middle of Rye Beach Road 184
In Early Spring 185
Walking Through Woods in Early Spring 186
Life As a Real Dream 187
Waking to Myself 188
Driving Up the Ohio River on Route 2 in Late Fall 189
Falling and Rising 190

Seven: Our Intentions, Waking to It
Someone Somewhere 193
Summer Visit 195
Listening to Tich Nyat Hanh on the Road to Detroit 197
Saying Farewell 199
Autumn Visit 200
Sitting on the Porch of a Friend's Cabin Along Chapel Creek 201
Walking the Labyrinth in Early Fall 202
The Aftermath 203
Where You Are 204
The Turnings 205
Drumming 206
Tasting the Day 207
Reconciliation 208
The Poetry Readings 209
Following the Road 210
Waking to It 211
Celebrating Lao Tzu's Birthday at the Taoist Healing
    Center in Cleveland, Ohio 213
Mourning the Death of My Taoist Healer 215
Brothers and Sisters 216
Doing a Drop-In Visit the Day After Christmas 217
Branches in a Stream 218
The Laboring 219
Retirement 220
Traveling Home 221

The Change 222
Satori Walking 223
Sleeping with the Remote 224
Secret Sharer...225
Just Sweeping..226
Bellingham Breakfast..227
Our Touch 228
Without Wind..229
The Bonds of Work 230
Sunday Service in the Ohio Valley 231

One: After

[Poems written after retirement
and reading the T'ang poets]

Returning
After T'ao Ch'ien, 365-427)

When I return to the college halls
where I taught for thirty years,
I meet the faces hurrying along
their heads full or filling—
a stream I swam for decades.

I have come to gather my mail,
carry boxes of books back home.
I move a slow shadow along the walls,
wishing everyone well.

Am I a fisherman without a hook,
or a field hawk gliding through clouds?

Not looking towards tomorrow always,
I settle in, breathe my life whole again.
Ask myself how it ever could be less?

(3/1/2003)

Visiting My Sister in Southeast Ohio in a Snowstorm
(After Hsieh Ling-Yun, 385-433)

I rise early, drink their coffee at the stove,
eat a plate of eggs and toast,
then go out to shovel snow banks,
try to slide my car back up their drive.
Too lazy to park it right last night,
I lift snow now down to gravel.
On the fourth try, I swing it back
up onto the crest of road, wave goodbye
to my sister robed at the window.

The roads are covered with three inches,
and so I creep along the ridge,
lose control at the dip before the trees,
find myself again on the other side.
Her road ends in an embankment—
my mind and body holding back,
no one to ask or blame—
I go on against windshield snow
sliding as I turn onto the main road.

These Appalachian foothills
have become strangers with rugged faces.
In harsh weather, nothing's tame.
No way to stop this change and loss,
I let go the stories of our lives,
hold the wheel loose yet steady,
become the road I'm on.

At the crest of Washington Hill,
I look down the steep Ohio Valley
to old Steubenville all snow covered,
the long Ohio at its foot.
I take a breath and swallow,
pump the brakes, ease forward
no way to hold it back.

(3/3/2003)

Climbing the Knob Through the Trees in Early Spring
(After Men Hao-Jan, 689-740)

The way up the hill leads through the trees
spread out like a farm of wilderness.

As a boy I walked here with friends
finding the path through green weeds
till we came to the tall spreading oak,
its tire swing hanging from a cable.
Someone would grab the rope and pull it back,
then swing out over a valley stream—
our breath held full in our chest
till we let it out in a yell for life.
One by one we would drop off
into the waiting stream, bathed in sun.

A man of sixty now,
with my own children grown,
I sit on this rock in leafy shade
stare at the thin trunk of a maple
that becomes my own thoughts.
And the sunlight through leaves
is the way beyond words.

                              (3/6/2003)

Standing at the Lookout at Sheldon's Marsh
(After Wang Wei, 701-761)

Toward the bay a blue sky
where lone white clouds drift.
Eight turtles on a log
lift their heads out of water.
Crickets and wood thrush
answer through leaf turning wind.
I sit inside the sound
my glasses folded in my lap.
At the point a snowy egret
spreads its wings.

(3/9/2003)

Driving Back Home in Late Winter
(After Li Po, 701-762)

We follow the Ohio down the valley
splitting the earth.

The road by-passes the mill town
where once a thousand families lived.

We get gas, and so take the old road
down the empty streets—

Cold black windows of storefronts,
neon lights now dead.

A few people stand on street corners
their hands hanging at their sides.

They look out under gray skies
at the slow cars passing by.

My wife and I grow quiet
at these once familiar streets.

Back on the highway toward home
we drive past bare trees.

The power here is drained by dam gates,
stolen by tall stacks of coal smoke.

Over on Brown Island
a dozen deer eat what grass remains.

Walking at Old Woman's Creek with a Friend
(After Wei Ying-Wu, 737-792)

You a mechanic waiting for work,
I a teacher retired after thirty years,
we walk the trail of fallen leaves,
look out in stillness across the pond
into the forest of trees.
An eagle's scree, then he appears
circling the pond's edge,
his wings a glide of emptiness
in the clean and steady air.
Old carp split the waters below.

Freed even of our names,
our minds a flow of idleness
we speak slowly of our lives,
turn memories into stories and back again—
A long way off and long ago…
soon vanish into sounds of water
lapping at the shore.

(3/12/2003)

At Home in a Time of War
(After Meng Chiao, 751-814)

A ragged snow like old laundry
lines the streets and yards.

A chorus of sorrow hangs in air
with the morning's news.

Our soldiers killing their soldiers
killing our soldiers over land and fear.

No count of women and children and aged
whose bodies are treated with bombs.

Work becomes another form of sleep
touching others with hungry eyes.

Lake ice splits open a thousand times
as the bodies of battles rise.

Wind chimes under grey clouds,
the cry of geese overhead.

Here in the village we hang a peace sign
on our door for passing traffic.

I close my eyes to remember summer
and the sounds of mourning doves.

(2/26/2003)

Lake Country in Early Morning

(After Han-Shan, 7th-9th century)

No wind as the evening birds
gather at the feeder.
I rise with the autumn moon
pale through the trees
walk down to the lake.

Edges of snow along the street
the taste of spring inside the air.
Passing quiet houses, I near the shore.
Broken ice meets the sky.
This lake country so flat
it creeps inside you,
day turning into night.

Winter Snow at Sunrise
(After Po Chü-I, 772-846)

While morning light opens and spreads
I walk with my old dog through new snow.
It rises to his chest, yet he leaps through.

I carry a white envelope to the mailbox,
knock snow off its lid, and drop it in.
No tracks yet in the snow,
everyone waking to its silence.

A cardinal there in the bushes,
a dozen starlings above in the trees.
We stand a long time measuring stillness
then turn back on the path toward home.
Me to my warm cup of coffee,
he to his bowl of food.
Later I will lay pieces of toast
across the snow in the yard.

                                        (2/18/2003)

By the River at Dusk
(After Po Chü-I, 772-846)

I've given up the struggle for recognition
fame and power an illusion too dear to maintain.
I wander at dusk to the river to fish,
my pole hanging in wind without bait.
I light my lantern along the weedy shore
watch the light bouncing low over waters.

A long barge passes, empty and homeless.
Through tall reeds a woman with red hair
kneels to wash her hands in the stream,
then lifts her soft voice in a song of love.
Who dares speak of more than this?
In idle ways my life stretches on.

(2/17/2003)

Walking a Field into Evening
(After Po Chü-I, 772-846)

For learned books, I read the grasses.
For reputation, a bird calls my name.
I cross a stone bridge with the pace of dusk.
And the meadow gate, six cows meditate.

For decades I ran with my mind up hill and down;
now idleness lets me see what is near.
An arrow of wild geese crosses the sky,
my body still, my feet firm on the ground.

(2/18/2003)

wild geese and mourning doves.
Words fly through us
as things affirmed.
A quiet sets into the night.
A mother kneels to welcome her child
into this circle of friends. And we all glow
in her young face, our blood warmed
by fire and wind. The stars above,
the earth below, we sing and sway,
join each other in birth again.

Looking Out onto My Back Porch in the Middle of Winter
(After Po Chü-I, 772-846)

A light snow falls fresh over the old.
The bamboo wind chime wears a white cap.
Rocks in the garden have aged through a long winter cold.
Someone has placed one in the wooden shrine
where we burn candles into autumn.
The houses nearby rest in a long silence.
Even the birds are hidden away.
I let out my dog, who steps around
the dry stones of his leavings.
He hunkers down like a statue,
then raises his head to the wind.

Somewhere a long way off
nations are deciding to go to war.
Men are talking loudly in a bright room
tasting fear in their water, lacking all sense
of the stillness gathered here.

                                    (2/15/2003)

The Call

(After Po Chü-I, 772-846)

I wake to a dog
barking out in the yard,
early light fringing the curtains,
in the other room, my wife's footsteps.

Let the newspaper
freeze in the yard.
An idle mind
is clear in the dawn.

I rise easy out of bed
my feet kissing the carpet
yesterday's clothes
hung on the chair.

The dog rushes in,
panting from yard wind,
and I walk out to
meet her face again.

(2/15/2003)

Early Rising
(After Chia Tao, 779-843)

My wife asleep in the covers,
only the sound of coffee
before the newspaper arrives.

Cold and dark outside,
the Azalea curls tight.
My dog stands at his bowl.

Under lamp light, I kiss my wife farewell.
In coat and gloves, step out onto frosted grass,
then drive without sound, under moonlight.
At the temple gate, I pull off the road.

I leave my car under a bare tree,
walk over quiet stones.
Treading through woods on frozen ground
I awaken birds roosting in trees.

By a pond I sit on an old log:
a bird call... a temple bell...
the colors of the dawn.

(2/21/2003)

Walking the Neighborhood into Night
(After Chia Tao, 779-843)

When you live along a lake
everything is flat,
and so we meet surprise
at the end of the street
in February, where the lake itself
becomes a landscape of ice.

The wind sneaks inside our collars
pushes our hands into their pockets.
Yet we stand here a long time
my wife and I facing it,
while I think of a hundred reasons
for turning back.
This is our walk before supper
and I know we'll return
to her warm rice and crab cakes.
I'll make coffee for desert,
and we'll talk soft in the living room
of things that matter.

They'll be no climbing of mountains,
no sailing of seas tonight,
only what rises inside us
as I nestle beside her,
feel the smooth curve
of her back.

(2/21/2003)

Visiting a Friend Along the Lake

(After Chia Tao, 779-843)

Your trailer lies
by the tracks before the lake,
yet you do not ride
or eat the fish.

Your flannel shirt
is soft from wear;
your leather coat
hangs from a hook.

Volumes of fine books
line your wooden block shelves;
your table is covered
with stacks of papers.

The coffee you offer
is strong but cold.
It tastes of your labor
to keep the place clean.

Last time you told me
of a girl you loved;
this time of your need
to move away.

We listen to rain on the roof,
finish our coffee,
then go out and try
to start your car.

(2/23/2003)

Rite of Passage at Sheldon's Marsh
(After Tu Mu, 803-853)

A red fox submerged in a pond legs down
drowned last night under a full moon,
so beautiful it stills my heart.

At the shoreline a snowy egret
stares into the emerald waters, lifts his wings
and body above the trees.

(4/2/2003)

Mount Tremper Before Dawn
(After Su Tung-Po, 1037-1101)

A temple bell through mountain mist—
I watch for footprints in the grass,

cross the wooden bridge before the others.
In still air I hear myself breathe.

Outside the temple door
I rest on granite steps.

Soaked lilac bend at my neck.
All the windows are dark inside.

Only the crows know my thoughts,
fly up at first light.

(3/30/2003)

Late Afternoon in Early Spring
(After Tu Fu, 712-770)

Lying on the back porch glider
I close my eyes to feel my breath,
count the sounds and their distances:
a dog bark—a train whistle—bird song in wind.

I drift back into the emptiness,
the greater life of sun and moon.
I rest a long time, then sleep,
wake to white petals of light.

Two: Cut and Stacked, Tanka and Haiku

[Japanese form poems in American English
Tanka: 5 lines of 5/7/5 7/7/
and Haiku: 3 lines of 5/7/5]

Heart Beat Tanka

Morning light comes on
paler at the rim of earth,
houses through the trees.

Driving all night toward home
my thoughts flatten with the road.

★★★★★★★★★★★

Full moon last night
sky a cobalt blue, clouds white
as a memory:

Walking home from her house
my cheeks flush with passion.

★★★★★★★★★★★★

A student tells me
he can't take my Zen class
because his plate is too full.

Walking in sun, I smile,
"Maybe Zen can empty it."

★★★★★★★★★★★★

After days in bed
I get hair cut in the rain
a woman strolls by.

The barber runs her fingers
through the hair along my neck.

Bellingham Walk January #2

Down the mountain path
wet stones and leafy ferns
all the way to the beach.

We baptize the new baby
with cool water and clear light.

The wet gingko leaf
fans across the sandstone
in a tincture of rain and wind.

The texture of our skin
thin lines to hold us in.

Splash of mountain stream
fresh snow melt rushing down
under wooden bridge.

Along the blue Pacific
we stand near Cedar bark.

Back home his father
holds him wrapped in blankets
while mother runs water.

He bathes in liquid warmth,
his face aglow like sun.

Walking Walden Pond

I walk round Walden
along the mossy roots of trees
circling Thoreau's waters.

Hard earth spread with pine needles
and no trace of footprints.

Where I walk, he walked,
and talked with birds, fish, and trees,
clear figure in the landscape.

Along the shoreline I look out
a figure in canoe drifts towards me.

A mist rises and glides
across the mirror of lake
morning birds waken.

A train rumbles, the wind sighs,
all of it wordless, but for this poem.

Morning light upon the pond
muted by low-hanging clouds
water lapping at the logs.

I sit on a stump and drink
sweet air in slow measured cups.

The leafy shade—
a few crows—a gray squirrel—
two fishermen in a boat.

Before me a day just begun
and no place to be but here.

Sheldon's Marsh Preserve

A long walk down a road
to a meadow through a gate
where wilderness rises.

The sound of leaves we kick
near meadow pond before dusk.

Berry bush and thickets,
tall grass, twisting willow and sassafras
bright telegraph of birds.

Wild ducks along an inlet—listen
to the lake, the falling of the leaves.

Walking Tanka

I walk out to it
the lone willow at the point
and it's always there

feet rooted in water
hair filled with summer rain.

At the creek's edge
a cement railroad bridge
crosses above

fishing here for hours
counting trains crossing over.

Have I lived this long
to be surprised by starlings
rising from a field?

At my door's closing, they lift in mass
beat the air in place, without song.

Weeds grow between the logs
stacked like loaves on the shelf
sleeping where they lie.

The memory of the oak
we carry in our bodies.

Driving West

Just north of Elkhart—
deer on the highway—
I pull back, hit the brakes.

My machine pull towards fate
His animal leap towards life.

Four horses in a wet field
rain dripping off their bent heads—
Nowhere to go.

The farmer sleeps by his warm wife
dreaming of ploughing spring earth.

Bare arms of apple trees
reaching out in all directions
for a spring sun.

Barren and wet they wait
their hundreds of children

Cows sitting in a field
like meditating rocks
Silence in the wind…

Their stomachs all that's working
on this Indiana farm.

Mingo Tanka

A light rain spreads itself
over the valley and the river—
sparrows under the eaves.

Last night a dog barked itself
into my dreams of home.

Outside, a window pane
reflects a cloud laden sky—
too cold for shirt sleeves.

A widow stands on her porch
sweeping the birds away.

3/20/2004

After Yoga

On mats before open doors
we stretch into long breaths
flowing music at dusk.

Outside the calls of wild geese
accent the distances.

Tanka Dog

Mad brushing of feet
across carpet in the night—
dog caught again

inside a seizure
running wildly home.

The dog at my feet
lies panting on the rug, fighting
a seizure to his brain.

He can no longer hear or smell
and his eyes call my name.

Shoreline

Beach stones and shells
inside footprints each wave
washes over.

Gulls cry winging white bodies
across the deepening blue.

A thousand birds
vanish across a blue sky—
each path erased.

We cross wet fields
under the same sun.

The stones beneath the tree
are mixed with winter leaves
I scrape away.

Sunlight falls across them now—
turning granite to gold.

On a river at dusk
thirty-seven white egrets
glide into the trees

Till...no river, no white birds,
no moon rising through trees.

Tanka Sequence After the Poet Saigyo

Half awake this morning
I look out to a new bird—
perched on the feeder.

Its wings streaked black and white
And on its white breast—a heart.

Sun through stained glass
as I sit in the church pew—
dirt under my nails,

new brick borders the garden—
acts more real than words.

Moon at day break
leaves worn out from
tossing all night,
a memory of something
too far to recall.

Sweeping the blossoms
of our magnolia tree
from the stone garden
I catch the first maple seeds
in my hair.

A cardinal
from high in the trees
calls at dusk
and my old dog
rises to be let in.

At the county landfill

two swallow drink from a puddle
then circle fresh trash bins
searching what we've brought:
sun high and no wind.

After three days
on the mountain trail,
a stubble of gray.
I place a dry branch
onto the fire.

One by one they come
torn from the evening sky,
thirty white egrets
landing in trees along the river,
turning gray with the night.

I dig around the bird feeder
roots thick as dog hair
seeds under finger nails.
and above the trees
the chatter of Cardinals.

All day the rumble and whine
of grass cutters and chemical sprays
controlling the lawn and trees,
till evening comes when birds sing
and crickets chirp through the night.

Haiku for Jack

Dust floats through sun—
where elbows press old flannel
into the wooden bar

His thick hand across
the glass, traps a summer fly
then lets it go.

Fetching canned peaches
motor oil on basement floor
her glasses in a drawer.

The cat falls asleep
watching him drain the afternoon
dreaming of women and trains

He picks up a book
props open the window—
sparrows in the yard.

Four guys on choppers
climb his porch steps and knock
as he pulls the shades.

The priest at the bar
stares into his glass and sighs,
"His heart just gave out."

Bellingham Walk January #1

Down the mountain path
my daughter carries her baby
wrapped in warm blanket.

We step across a stream
water so clear the stones lay
golden at our feet.

Wet leaves and pine needles
Nature's living carpet
going back to earth.

We have come out
to greet the mountain spirit
look out over long waters.

In the bay
below the bluff
a rainbow of kayak.

Smells of spruce and cedar
become a part of us—
I step back with camera:

Wife and daughter, grandchild, all
his small face and hands showing
another kind of Nature's light.

Driving Down Ohio Route 13

Five black and white ponies
bend to the cool moist grass
as sun warms their backs.

A green horse trailer
beside an old red barn
horses in a field.

Rising on fields of
quiet cows and moist lambs
the sun eats the dew.

A man bends over
like a crane in his garden
plucking summer dill.

On the road to class
the raccoon I swerve to miss
saves the day.

Walking Haiku

Above the birds
the hoot and rumble
of the train.

Outside the lime shed
along the tracks to the spring
hoof prints of young deer

Sun passes overhead
moss clings to shingles
a dog barks to be let in.

Cool spring water
poured into the cup
of your hands.

Along the trail
wild blueberries underfoot
nowhere to hide.

Pebbles scatter underfoot
as we walk the morning trail
searching trees for birds.

Remembering
a pile of pale Gingko leaves
gathered for a tincture.

Drop hook in water
lie back and listen through waves—
doing nothing well.

Tent flaps blowing
cattails bending to the stream
eating fish for days.

Reading the board face
a tale of generations
rough against the hand.

Bones and feathers
lying in the creek brush—
snowy egrets overhead.

Branches like storm rags
lie in the yard; stems like arrows
stuck deep in mud.

The path up the hill
rises with my breath—
no news to carry.

Falling light
a window of trees
handfuls of leaves.

I toss a stick
upon the quiet waters
of this pond.

Wild geese white and gray
turn in winter sky
doing this for years.

Subway Haiku

On the subway
her tan shoulder in the sun
a hundred colors.

She glides down
onto her cushion, wet hair
against her neck.

Blizzard winds shake wires
icicles fall to the ground—
footprints in the snow

The dog shivers
in the crusted snow
dropping his logs.

Across the thick snow
I carry a new television
into the house.

Coffee
in a white mug
the radio on.

The screech of cats
at two a.m.—
birds again at seven.

At Home Haiku

Sparrows scatter at feeder
chased by five black grackle
chased by a Cooper's hawk.

Red spider mite
spins itself across
my page.

Baby scooting back
over carpeted floors—
hot rice sits in bowls.

Packed in so tight
these books of mine
are making love.

Reaching my hand
inside the cereal box
only crumbs to eat.

Lying on the porch swing
counting the cars that pass
beneath a purple sky

Young woman jogging
beside the road, your hair
in sun, aflame.

Evening light through sea grass
golden leaves turn softly
touching the mind.

The dog pants in rain
mud crusted on his paws
claws to be let in.

After hours of turning soil
I stop to take a leak—
sink shovel in wet earth.

my father's ratchet set
in a rusted box
waiting.

Random Haiku

Reading poems aloud
in my motel room
learning by heart.

The bobcat paces
inside his leafy cage—
outside the cry of birds.

Clatter of plates
and words, waiting
for the check.

Fall leaves overhead
and below the water's face
oars stroking down and through.

Into Still Air

The sounds
of magnolia blossoms
falling

Yard birds
gather to feed
again

A cardinal sings
in the moist air
of spring

A lawnmower
in my neighbor's yard
rests.

Words
can't touch
it.

Three: Native Grounds, What Is Near

Ohio Valley Vision

I borrow a piece of clothesline
from my mother-in-law's basement
to walk my dog in the old neighborhood.

Avoiding Miller's dogs, we turn down an alley
past the leaning flaps of garage,
the recent rubble of back yards.

At each we meet a Beagle in a cage
or barking on an angry chain.
At the corner an old woman
yells, "Keep away from there!"

Yet we walk on, cross the cinder-covered street
melting through last week's snow.
A red pickup nearly runs us down.

This town is like an old wound,
and I shake my head, tell the dog
we are headed home, when there appears

before a white frame house
in a tree clipped of all its limbs——
a cement statue of St. Francis
whose arms are lifted
that all birds may sing.

Our House on Murdock Street

"Acts of sacrifice make sacred the earth."
N. Scott Momaday

Our house was never
more than that. Our yard
was never a lawn. We
cut the grass with a push mower
every two weeks.
We painted the eaves when they
blistered and peeled.
In winter
we hauled our ashes
out to the alley. We swept
the porch each week.

                    Inside
things were kept casual
but clean. At night
the counter would be
cleared, our shoes thrown
into the closet, our beds
made the way we'd left them.

And yet we got by
taking what we had
to pay the bills
for four kids.
Dad worked two jobs—
railroad and furnaces.
Mother cared for us, kept
food on table, read us
books at bedtime,
that's how
we got by.

And this...

When our friends

came over, Mom would
feed them, listen to
our stories, dance along
to our music.
                I remember
the first week
of my father's
two week vacation
he spent planting
saplings along the highway
across the street.

What more does it take?

What Is Near

I pass my mother aproned at the stove
who turns to wave a wooden spoon
fresh from cabbage soup, and I go down
into the basement smell where my father
stands at his lathe cutting sounds.

We nod, do not speak, await
what is to come—the wood's shape.

At the workbench I search the wooden drawers
for bolts and nuts that fit. I tighten the vise,
spin a wing nut down its shank, nothing more than this
in the whir of spinning wood.

This is the standing beside, each of us—
the finding of our way.

Along the Ohio

Frost rises along the tracks,
white feathered branches in the light.

Blue barges of coal
work their way up river
past houses sleeping late
through Sunday morning.

Backyard sparrows
line the wooden fences
awaiting bread crumbs.

Thin plumes of chimney smoke
rise straight to the sky.

Business as Usual—Ohio Valley

A dog barks in a neighbor's backyard while the garbage truck pulls up the alley. Sun is beaming off the white vinyl siding as cars rush up and down the hill. It takes a certain momentum to go anywhere around here.

Last night Ralph the furnace man came over at 9 pm to check my mother-in-law's air conditioner. I held the flashlight, then offered him a cup of coffee.

This morning my wife and Sue have gone off to have her hair 'done' at Jeanette's Beauty Shop down on Commercial Avenue.

The backs of those buildings face the railroad tracks that run along the river. I've seen them from inside the mill as trains pulled ladles of hot slag and liquid steel along the huge blast furnaces. "Dinosaurs" they call them now. The roar and clash of it all is almost too much. Smoke rises to the pale skies; a flame torches the excess gas overhead. It's a continuous cast operation—a century of working round the clock in shifts.

On the hills are nested red brick schools, raising our children to something more, another kind of labor, lifting with the mind.

Outside my window, the mill-gray pigeons perch on power lines.

Filling in the Background

How many ways can you stare at a photo?
How many ways can you not see what's there?

My mother's high school graduation photo:
her pretty face, and soft, clear eyes.
Wearing her best dress, hair combed smooth,
she looks out toward a life to come:
all the houses and children, dogs and cars,
a million meals and laundry baskets
the countless books and television shows
late into the night—a hundred thousand suns
a hundred thousand moons. What else?
The letters from an unforgiving mother,
long phone calls from her friends,
Her cats, one after another.

She looks out through it all
trusting, uncertain, gently smiling.

We know now that she must have been
pregnant then with my older brother.
My father's strong hands and deep eyes.

Rock and Rolling in the 1950's

"Don't forget where you came from."
　　　　—A working-class oath.

We were two high school rock groups
briefly merged into one in a
small industrial town.

The Vibrations and the *Fidels*,
our names spelled out the dream.
The Vibrations grew out of band camp
jamming in the men's barracks,
playing while whirling majorettes
danced before the bonfire.
The Fidels had crooned doo-wop
in locker room showers, bounced
their sound off restroom tiled walls.

After a month of practicing
in family basements and garages,
we were ready for our first gig.
So we worked extra hours
as ushers and fry cooks,
or borrowed money from our families
to buy the matching shirts—
maroon long sleeves—
at Weisberger's Clothing downtown.

Our big gig was a sock hop
at the "Wigwam" Community Center.
We came early to set up:
two amps, two mics,
three guitars, and a set of drums.
We were our own roadies;
someday we might have our groupies.
Out in the back alley
we smoked our last cigarettes.
Police cruisers gleamed in the parking lot,
kids played under street lights a block away

as the mills roared and the night Bessemer
spread its orange-pink light.

At ten after the hour, we were introduced,
and so strolled out of the back room
in our new shirts, to a shower of hometown applause.
Friends and enemies gathered
to measure our sound.
And we had it that night—
playing our eight songs
from somewhere deep inside,
without really trying, in that
easy effort of riding a wave.
Our intention lay in each note,
each beat, each chord change.
It echoed off the walls, and
sunk into the dancing bodies.
Doo-wop and rock and roll,
rockabilly and rhythm and blues,
we played it all, lifting ourselves
and our town above the noise and dirt.
It rocked and rolled right out of us.
We were part of that dream.
We were taking it home.
We were making it real.

Working the Steam Table with Darlene

I change quickly in the men's john,
stand before the mirror more white
than the porcelain and tile.
First day on the steam table
I watch and listen, breathe in
hot smells of grease and ham.
Dolly hums beside me, shifts her weight
to cut and butter toast; calls,
"Order up, Honey" to the waitress
with the red bow in her hair.

Suddenly Darlene backs out of the kitchen
hoisting a pan of macaroni and cheese.
With a metal spoon she flips out an empty,
drops the new one into place,
reaches past me for a lid.
I am less than useless standing here.

"Get an apron, Honey," pointing to a tub of
drowned potatoes sliced like fingers,
"We'll blanch some fries."
Darlene shows me once, "First
you take a handful of these"
then tossing them into the wire basket
she lowers them into the angry fryer,
"Three minutes—no more, no less."
Above the popping grease, she boasts,
"We still fry our own."

Two minutes into the job, I catch her
watching me. She almost smiles
pulling me aside, "Don't stand over it.
You'll melt."

My smile is wasted as she bends
to draw out a tray of Jello.
"We'll set these up on plates with lettuce leaves,
then top with whip cream. Fill that tray."

Those rings that people work,
she works around me.
Juggling Jello squares,
while she fills orders at the table,
I know the lie of male sufficiency.
And I can't help noticing how the Jello
is red as her lips. Her hair
is pulled back tight and colorless.
Her body trim and strong, her bare arms
clear and young; she is twice my age
yet moves in perfect readiness.

By noon I am tossing fish and fries
onto plates, then out onto the
steel counter, where waitresses grab them,
shake their heads, till Darlene takes me aside,
"Be gentle with the food...
or it loses its taste."
Nodding to the tables she sighs,
"The food comes first, not the waitresses"
and I look into her quick blue eyes, hear:
"Only work as fast as you can....
No faster....Understand?"

At two I lean against the counter
as the head cook walks behind, and
Darlene touches my arm to whisper,
"Never stand around....
Always clean," and I do
the rest of the afternoon.

At three I bend at her knees
to count the Jellos; my head
grows dizzy with it all.
Elbows deep in food, I have
eaten nothing all day but Darlene.
Who is this woman
teaching me of work,
what my father could not?

We stand together at our table smelling
of the same food. She serves herself.

At four I punch the clock
exchange my clothes again
read the story of stains
upon my shirt.

Working It Out

For Janet

I sit in the university hall
and hear a woman my age
speak her working class life.
This morning the hall is too large.
yet the light falls golden
on her face.
"It's been a journey," she says,
"One carried on inside." And I know
she knows the silent pain.
"I am working class," she says.
"And I am not working class."
Her truth bites into me
as she brushes back her dark hair
and smiles.

"We begin in sharp location
and travel forward by denial," she
says. "We leave our working roots
to enter Middle Class and feel
a fraud in both." I am nodding
toward my coffee cup,
my own familiar hands.
I have dug track with these,
drove truck, fished streams, and yes,
sat in an office pecking the keyboards
of computer screens.

My eyes rise to hers
as she opens herself:
"I won the company scholarship.
If my father hadn't worked for them
I might not have gone, and he
might not have died so young."
She breathes inside the wake
of that emotion as we all
feel our guilty clothes.

"I am working class, and
I am not," she says again.
And I think of my own father
whose shower time wasn't on the clock,
so he drove home to my mother
and us kids, washed in the basement—
emerged into the kitchen light.
Did they have to think
that they were working class? Do I?

I know their sacrifice was never
meant to bind me. My own children
who love to visit grandparents
have never known the mill's insides,
never seen the pick ax come down
to start the day around. I stand
like my immigrant grandparents
a foot in both worlds. Double vision.
"I am and I am not."

This woman speaks our life,
tells how we somehow held the world
closer because we knew early
that it was broken and
therefore precious.
She comes around the podium
to spread the words before us
to say how we must accept
no definition but ourselves.
"Our community as working people
holds our strength. We are
the working force." She stops
and we go on, applauding her,
a sister's face, and my own heart
leaps with glad relief.

Where I Am Going/Where I Have Been

Outside the mill gate
I wait for my dead father
to come out and raise his arm
in salute to the fifteen years
since we last spoke.

He will be wearing his brakeman's clothes
dark jacket and pants shedding dirt,
his work gloves folded inside his cap.

And I will glide the car forward,
wave to his tired but smiling face,
and he will open the door and get in.

Wordless we will drive along the river,
the car's engine the only voice.

At the traffic light before the bridge
we will read each other's faces,
touch the space inside our hearts.

His hands will be rough and read like road maps
all the way home.

Driving Toward Home

I had driven half the day
down long hot roads
to these Appalachian hills
rising out of Ohio flatlands.
I wound down my windows
to the coolness of the forest
along green rolling streams.

Above the highway, box houses
nestled on clay ridges.
The road had become a song
a leaning toward freedom
amidst old tobacco farms.

Outside the Coffee Cup restaurant
a wasp flew into my car
and buzzed around the dome light
till I swept him out with my cap
holding firm to the brim.

Inside the cool darkness
the long looks of strangers
took me in, till I seated myself
at the counter. A gray haired waitress
handed me a paper menu, smiling
"Honey, what can I get you to drink?"
I drew a long breath of home
pointed to the pot in her hand,
"Well, how 'bout a cup of that?"

Reunion at Cross Creek

Walking down the hills of home
to the near side of the river,
a light snow in morning sun.

Back at the house people rising
taking hot showers, combing hair,
eggs turned to suns on plates.

I have gone out to a place
where we once fished along a creek:
The whisper of traffic overhead
on the bridge near the tracks.
A dozen starlings root among leaves
on the frozen bank.

I close my eyes over forty years
and my brother appears on the other side
bending to light us a fire,
Let's see what's biting here, he says,
We'll go home in a little while.

I sit on a log counting breaths
disappearing in the snowy dawn.

3/20/2004

Mingo Junction—December 2002

for Guy Mason

I walk down the morning hill
past the blank faced houses
leaning in the wind,
to visit an old friend.
And we walk the empty streets
of our hometown—
dark storefronts cold as glass.

We talk the weather of memories.
Beyond the orange of mill gate steps
we enter the Town House bar—
cozy quarters for home folks,
a juke box of country tunes
old oak bar along the wall.
We meet faces of the past
warn and warm, and I nod
as my friend connects the names.
Hands go out across the years.

We sit with our eggs and toast
bring coffee to our lips
and our words go back and forth
between today and then—
stories of classmates, thoughts of politics,
the way the world keeps going wrong,
things we hold on to.

Back on the streets
we walk to Minch's.
My friend opens the door front
to a room full of men my dad's age.
"You're Deb Smith's boy.
Your old man worked the railroad in Weirton,"
they ask and answer.
I shake hands again and again
with these storytellers of my town.

Then we enter the "back room"
where men my age—retired now—
read my face, think memory.
"Smitty, yeah, how's your brother?"
"Okay, and how's your Mom?"
In a while the play will begin,
cards slapped down,
chips cast out, drawn in.
It is a rite as old as men and this town.
We stand around, then say so long,
duck out the door. Snow falling lightly
in the streets of our mill town.
Two friends embrace
for all the years.

Dreaming of Home

In my dream, the old bus station
is still open; the dusk of streets
meets the lights I enter.
The clack of pool balls,
guys playing 9-ball in the other room.
The same wooden benches
brushed by skirts and trousers
a hundred thousand times.
Memory mixes loss with hope
like an old car I think I've found.
And I look up for a sign
reach inside my pocket for my ticket.

An ancient poem tells us
to let go of the past
as well as the future
to be in the present,
yet I am here now
inside this dream.

A young boy sits with his mother
who strokes his fresh cut hair;
a man stands at the lunch counter
staring into the eyes of the lone waitress,
cigarette smoke rising from his lips.
The old guy at the ticket window
gazes out at the others—
all of us quiet, all softly present,
and I am each and all.

The book of Tao
teaches us not to grasp
not to make our lives into a story,
yet these images are real
as stones inside the heart.

A bus comes by and people rise
walk out into the evening street.

I follow to the bus door
then step up into the glow:
the others facing forward:
my uncle and aunt, grandma,
the neighbor kid who died.
I nod to each, then take my seat,
no thought of what I've done
with my life. I try to read our destination.
The door closes and we are moving
gliding forward into night.

To the Silence of Men

I'm doing it again, mixing my cereals
the way my father used to do
standing in the kitchen in work clothes
before we rose for school. I know
because I came to rise with him
those summers I worked the mill…silent
at the table while he brewed his tea,
mute language of our bodies as we
moved alone into the day together.

His letting the dog out, my laying
slices of ham on white bread, folding
the wax paper so at the ends, placing
two each in our lunch pails, with
whatever fruit we had, watching the
clock hands, gathering up our hard hats
from the closet, going out the door
silent together, the way I do now
with my son, home from work, tired
and trusting, swallowing the words.

The Bridge to Steubenville

I walk out at dusk, halfway across Market Street Bridge,
stare down through the steel grating to the river
gliding below my feet, the light of mills spreading
a film of knowing drifting through memory.
A truck rolls by me disappearing into West Virginia's dark hills.
And in Ohio, streetlights of a city abandoned by the weak and
    moneyed;
families huddled in living rooms, their newspaper a frozen lump in
    the yard.
And these gray girders near my cheek, suspended wings
forged in the machines of mills, coal smoke rising into cold night air.
I have come out this night to know this—
the way this river moves on, the way it remains.

Four: **Standing in Muddy Waters**

Entering the Pain in Muddy Waters

Was that a leaf or a bird
I just ran over?

The radio cackles of an accident near home—
Could it be my son?

I watch the weather map
for my family and myself.

I mute myself through scenes
of people in Iraq, Liberia, Afghanistan...

A woman in the grocery store
slapped her son for talking loud.

My breath rises in my chest;
my shoulders tighten down.

I pull off the road
and feel the world's pain.

Like these lotus flowers
I must stand in muddy waters

bend with the winds or
harden till I break.

The bird inside my heart
still calls my name.

8/22/2003

A Father's Pain

My father ignored his pain,
rode it out without complaint—
high threshold they call it now.

He worked as a brakeman in snow and rain.
Once he pulled his own back tooth,
held the pain in his side one time
till it burst his appendix, then
lay in a hospital bed for days.

He wasn't hard on us kids,
never struck us, took us to
doctors and dentists when needed.
He used to sing in the car
bought us root beers along the road.
He loved us with his deeds.

The day he died, he played golf
in the morning, came home,
muffling the pain in his arm,
went upstairs and lay down.

Making My Hospice Visits

At the dementia ward, I find Gerty
sitting at table with her four friends
all of them mute before their food.
And I re-introduce myself
for the twentieth time, each looking
at me like a child awakened.
"I'm Larry. I'm here to feed you, Gerty."
She looks back and I pick up the fork.

> There are bridges down, wires blown away
> The silence of waiting, nothing to say.

Four women and I the only one talking
till there is just silence. Gerty looks up,
mayonnaise on her lips, and pats my hand
whispers, "Now you eat some of this."
Rules say I shouldn't. I explain,
"I'm the feeder now. I'm here to serve you."
Her eyes plead, "Go on. Eat half, please."
Truth is I just can't. "Please…" I beg, "Eat.
I'm your slave," and they laugh all around.

> There are lights inside the darkness
> windows still open to a breeze.

Last time I'd told them all how much
I enjoyed being there with them, then
when punching the door code to leave,
a man stepped in, saw me, and quick
pulled the door shut, before I could escape.
"No!," I protested. "I don't belong here."

> Sometimes when the light is right
> a window becomes a mirror.

I carry bits of food to her lips.
She takes them in, I wait.
I drop crumbs on her lap,

and she pretends not to notice.
Sometimes her hands flutter on her napkin
seeking to fold it straight.
She is my grandmother, my mother, my self.

Now her hand touches my own,
strokes the hair on my arm.
I hug her goodbye and she smiles.
She is dying of lung cancer and Alzheimer's.
Her eyes tell me she knows.
"I'll see you next week," I say and turn.
Always I struggle to come,
then find myself quiet in their eyes, made real,
yet am relieved to be going out
from the shadows into sun.

And who do we walk towards;
and who do we walk from?

I wash my hands at the sink
watch water swirl slowly down the drain.
Jane, the floor supervisor, comes in
and I tell her how Gerty didn't eat,
how she seems to be losing ground.
She looks back, touches me with her eyes.
"You know," she sighs into our silence,
"It won't get any better."
I breathe softly, then turn to go,
and she whispers, "Don't stop coming."

The Alchemy of Pain

For James

It is a Wednesday morning in January
and the snow has fallen through the night.
I lift thick shovels of it to clear a path,
for I would drive to visit a friend, new from a stroke.
As I drive the slippery roads, I tell myself,
I will find the words.
I will be myself.

I pass the New Delphi plant, turn right through the Projects
into Sandusky's Black neighborhoods.
Ebenezer Baptist Church on Pearce, then Clay Street,
a short right to an older stucco house,
across the tracks from the Amtrak station.
And as I park, I think—*I have never been here.*
I have never visited my friend James.
There is no good reason for this.

I walk the snowy pathway to the front door and knock.
Again. *Should I go around back?* I hear a footsteps,
then the door opens to his middle daughter.
"I've come to see James. I'm Larry, his friend."
She lets me inside—a big room. "I'll get him,"
she sighs still in pajamas, then disappears.
I am standing there a long time, family photos on the walls,
a tiny television in a chair, a newspaper on the floor,
against the wall leans a walker—*James's walker!*
I have not seen him since the stroke hit him
like a reckless car on a street corner sending him
to ICU, then on to Cleveland.
I begin to worry what he'll be like.

I sit in a plastic chair, unzip my coat, when suddenly
James is there, thin in white t-shirt,
smiling and walking towards me.
I rise, extend my arms, my hands widen in an arc,
"James it's you," I say, but think, *Lazarus!*
as he glides towards me. I take his hand,

hug his wounded body. "You look good, my friend—
You've been through so much."
"Yes," he says and nods, holding that silence
till memory grows. My own breath deepens as we sit,
close by window light, *We will be all right.*

I tell him he is missed by many.
He nods, "And how...are...you?"
he asks with slow deliberateness.
Always so articulate—he gives more of his eyes now
to carry meaning. He lets me talk, holds one chair arm,
in the other he rolls a few pennies.
"And how about you, friend?" I ask.
He looks down at his bare arms turned up
a dark trail where needles have been.
I nod into his eyes, his gentle smile,
"I've seen...better...days."
A pause follows every phrase—
which turns to an understanding shared.
In this new pace between us, I begin to
pick up his trouble with going on—
not with his life, but with thought.
As he reaches, it is gone—that word
to make clear and explain. Gone.
He repeats the same three words
again, again, but cannot go on, cannot grasp
or connect through empty space.
His thin face in pain, his eyes searching,
I nod, "I understand," even when I do not,
and so join him on this pathway into silence.

I tell him the story of my uncle
who came back from a stroke
gaining ground with each week.
He smiles, "You have...an...uncle?"
And I say, "No, he's gone." Silence,
and something moves me to stroke his arm.
He nods, looks into my eyes,
takes my hand. Two friends,
who used to rush with words,

branching thought electric,
now talk with silences. What can't be said
now between us understood.
And my own deep sadness flows through him
as I breathe softly, and it becomes
a quiet joy to have him back,
to sit here inside his house,
be with him still,
feel the losses slowly turn to gains.

The V.A. Medical Center

(Old friend, I witness your life, as I do my own.)

I go to visit a friend at the psychiatric ward, 52-A,
out at the edge of a Cleveland suburb.
A huge two-story structure of old orange brick and
reinforced windows runs around the campus green.
Inside the gates, I check my wallet for I.D.—
in case I have to get out.

Ray greets me with a handshake that I
turn into a male embrace. We both thought we had lost him.
Five weeks in the lock-down ward—a threat
to others or himself—who really knows?
We sit on a bench outside as he tells it again—
the ranting at his neighbor, the police at the door,
the storm of his arrest and being brought out here.
He's retold it a hundred times to prove he's not delusional.
I can't stop him, so he goes on—his long hair and recent beard,
his new glasses and clothes making me search for the real Ray.

He pauses to light up, and I ask about the food—*Good enough,*
he sighs. And the men? *Not bad,* he says, *but you have to watch your back,*
and another story ensues, his voice racing to keep up with his thoughts.
I try to listen but gaze out to the trees turning colors, releasing their leaves
in cool October wind. Twenty-five years I've known him—
yet this is the first lock-up, and probably not the last.

I want to slow my friend down, release the wild energy of his body
out into the autumn wind, but I cannot.
Yet he does slow as another outdoor-inmate approaches,
Can I get a light from you guys? his head held low.
Sure, Ray says, *I'm allowed to carry this weapon,*
and he whips out his lighter as a way of making friends.
We smile, and the other fellow sits at Ray's left. He hardly speaks
till Ray asks, *How long on lock-down?*
Two weeks is all he says, facing straight ahead
in a benign stare—victim of benign neglect.

Then I remember something and pull out the rubber snake
that my grandson sent to make Ray laugh. And he does,
laugh out loud and openly, so that the other guy and I
turn to each other, and I realize that he looks like me.
We are salt and pepper to Ray, three men on a bench,
each a veteran of life's struggles, all of us brothers.

Fading with the Night

My friend is fading into a darkness
of the mind, frenetic energy behind his eyes
blinds him to others and himself. His voice
is blocked by fear and rage
black bird of night draining all his
laughter and wit.

                Sitting in the yard
I stare at his face, his drunken hair,
hear his accusations swallowing himself.
I want to touch him in some way
to steady him, bring him back.
He borrows a light from another patient,
warns me not to trust that guy.

The sun is shining and it's raining in my heart.

We sit in silence, stare into the woods,
the darkness coming on.

Breakfast of Poets on Detroit Avenue

I drive through Route 6 fog
along Lake Erie's rocky edge
to see my friend Ray
at the Tower Cliff Apartments
across the Rocky River bridge.
He is standing on the corner
like a poet hitchhiker out where
I cannot miss him. I pull in
and hand him a basket of fruit
plucked this morning from IGA,
and a copy of *Poets & Writers*
with all their list of awards
neither of us ever wins.
Later we will scoff at them
drowning ourselves in coffee.

Ray smiles and jokes about the weather,
his lack of furniture. "No roaches though,"
he grins. Looking out at the parking lot
he says, "I'm thinking of collecting
grocery carts. Sell them on E-Bay."
On the coffee table are the cigarette rolls
he stuffs with tobacco from Cheap Smokes.
"Cuts the cost more than half," he says,
then coughs toward the window. His poetry books
stand in stacks along the wall like
prisoners or newspapers, fifty copies of each.
"It's good insulation," he grins
and we laugh, going out.

Walking dirty Detroit Avenue
past old shops, bars, and lighted cafés
we dodge the cars, dancing like
Gene Kelly in *Singing in the Rain.*
John's Diner on the corner
is full of smoke and regulars
crouched on stools sipping coffee
reading their news and eggs.

"Morning," the cashier smiles
"Sit anywhere," and we do
in a back booth along the wall.
A guy about 50 with short gray hair
sets down two glasses of water, the menus,
and speaks that one word, "Coffee?"
"Great," we both say, and
turn to each other—*Great minds...*

Ray orders the potato pancakes
with applesauce, and so do I—
When in Lakewood...
Before our food arrives we
talk about fellow poets—
Vladimir, Mike Gill, Christopher Franke,
Ray McNiece out on the road,
Daniel Thompson—Cleveland's poet of
the streets and poor—now gone.
Nothing much to say
except their names as if
to invite them to our table.

While we eat I look up through smoky windows
at the sun cutting through the fog.
I drink a slow cup of coffee;
Ray smokes another cigarette
and then reads me his new poem.

Reaching Out/Holding On

My friend snapped today after our visit.
He's telling me how he heard it like a spark
in his brain. He's calling his
two last friends and threatening us
with guilt at neglecting him. His voice
is distant across telephone lines.

This morning Ann and I entered his new place—
two wooden chairs and a table with the cigarettes
he rolls, his stacks of books, the television
he's afraid to watch, no couch, no mattress, and
yet he joked with us, talking fast as wind.

We went out to John's Diner on Detroit Road,
sat in smoke eating pancakes, but the talk
was good as he forgot his pain and told us
of his writing, ignoring his month
in the mental ward. We walked out into the cold air
like any other group of friends.

Back in his apartment he gave us
a knitted blanket for our pregnant daughter,
one he had saved for his own dream family,
our eyes avoiding that impossibility,
the hollow welling in my heart,
perhaps like the snap in his brain.

I don't know what it's like to
lose so much of yourself. My losses
all come slowly with age. He tells me now
how I put him down today, and I just listen
till his train of words runs down. I say,
"You will always be my friend," though
I no longer know what that means.
I want to look him in the eyes, reach
across the darkness to him, but he
no longer has any arms.

Letter to d.a. levy in Existential Heaven

d.a. levy, you were four months older,
yet I've outlived you by three decades,
and you know how hard that must have been.
You broke yourself for us, man, left us
to find our own songs for it.
Half your ashes at Whitehaven Cemetery,
the rest with family and friends,
your spirit spread over this cold city
that you loved more than I,
yet hated about the same.

West Side kid off Lorain Ave,
father a shoe salesman who
never measured your feet.
When you graduated from Rhodes High,
you wanted to kill yourself,
but found real books instead and art—
friends inside the darkness.
And you kept saving yourself with words
until you couldn't anymore.

Rebel artist, without a cause,
outliving James Dean by two long years.
You renounced everything, even yourself.
Your titles ring through my head at night:
"Egyptian" and "Tibetan Stroboscope"
"Junkmail Oracle," "North American Book of the Dead."
Did you confuse Buddha's emptiness
with the existential nothingness, that night
you put a bullet through your head?
We need our friends.

Whitman lover of the streets and coffeehouses,
the bars and book shops, beloved Asphodel,
leaving your tired and lovely Dagmar
asleep in East Cleveland apartment
to walk down to Euclid and take the hungry bus
to University Circle. It was a scene you made

and watched, writing the long nights
covering the cold city with your lines,
pumping the days away on your letter press,
spinning the mimeo machine, breaking yourself
to get the words out to a city that turned its back.
Judges and lawyers and real estate men
cutting up the scene for themselves.
Police banging on doors and heads,
busting you all for contributing to
their own delinquent kids.

You were slight in the city wind,
blown in off Lake Erie. With Levi's,
motorcycle boots, and dark beard,
you found comfort nowhere in myths and lies.
Cleveland Milarepa yogi, you
stood in Trinity Cathedral at "The Gate,"
and opened the hearts and eyes.

You kept happening, broke yourself
a thousand times to keep us alive.
But then you couldn't. And you passed
quickly through a cloud like Hart Crane
or Sherwood Anderson, or Kenneth Patchen,
offshore somewhere in the Ohio night.
Your life was a book you wrote then erased
leaving us to survive without you.
The year after you died they closed the Palace
and Euclid Beach Amusement Park,
and then the Cuyahoga River caught fire.

Entering the Pain

A young woman enters my office
and I sense the pain she carries
in her body and her eyes.
I rise and take her trembling hand.
She sits, says, "Thanks for coming in."
The light is soft on my cluttered office.
I am no therapist or counselor,
just a teacher-friend who has known cancer.
I say, "Thanks for sharing with me,"
and turn my chair to face her—
"Cervical cancer ... cone surgery ...
I'm only nineteen ... my mother died when I was two..."
Her shiny hair has been brushed a thousand times,
but not by the hands of her mother.

I sit and nod as her life unfurls.
"My father married again when I was nine.
My second mom died two years ago.
I know I've not dealt well with that."
I touch her arm, "You've dealt with so much,
and now you're dealing with this."
Her tears well as she looks ahead, "I know."
I tell her how it was for me too
hearing my biopsy over the phone,
swallowing my life. She looks up.
Our voices are real. Not the voices
of classrooms, or telephones,
just two people talking in a little room.
Her story goes on—of alcoholic parents,
leaving home at fourteen, no one to tell.

For half an hour I walk quiet
through the shadows of her life.
How could someone so small bear so much?
I say to her, "Listen, you are real.
You can't not have this cancer, but you can
still decide how you'll deal with it."
She sighs, "I feel I've lost control

of my life." Silence. Then I dare to say it:
"I'll tell you what cancer has taught me.
Those who would never lose, can never gain.
And so they never know that we aren't really broken.
Though we would block it with pretense and fear,
the heart is always open." And she
breaks open in tears, and I wait,
move close to hold her once—my own pain
pressed gently to me. "You are not broken,"
I say again, breathe deep, "Listen, you are more
than your pain, larger than all of this."
She sighs, looks into my eyes, "I know."
We talk more of her sharing this
with those she loves, and then she rises
gathers her books into her arms
and I whisper once for her, for me,
for all of us, "Love yourself,"
and she is gone.

The Alcohol Recovery House

A young child
  runs across the soft carpet
to her mother.

Grandma smokes alone
  on the front porch
inside the rain.

Sickness

A mother stands waiting
near the prescription counter
mind sleepless from
nursing her sick son
left at home with
her older child.

She gazes at the bottles
of vitamins and herbs—
Nothing is for sure
except this deep need.
Her eyes dull
and so she sits down
at the blood pressure machine.
What does it matter? she asks.
This baby alone is real—
If it vanishes
so do I.

An older man
touches her sleeve.
"Mind if I use that, honey?"
Her look tells all,
and he, "No, you rest.
I'll come another time,"
the first kind words in days.

This Day

For Kate and Bob

While visiting a Columbus library
I learn of my friend's cancer
from his wife standing strong,
though her voice trembles when she talks.
I take her hand, look into her eyes,
and do not ask how long.

On the drive home, I think of him:
born a week apart, brothers under the skin,
his fingers flying over guitar strings,
his voice telling us an old story.
I touch the warm pain of knowing,
then disappear into the road.

Towards home along the lake,
I look out to familiar fields of
wheat and corn in evening sun.
Beside me now—a great white egret—
its long body, its huge swooping wings,
glides through wordless air.

Writing in the Middle of the Night
For Bob

A friend a long way off
is passing through the
final stages of cancer,
a path he'd taken
years ago with his wife.
It comes and takes you,
turns your cells to purple gel.
He knows all that
as he lies tonight
cocooned from the consuming pain.

I am so speechless now
I can only send him peace—
all the cannabis plants of
Athens County during the 60's
when he wrote those wonder stories
of old farmers and tool salesmen
in those backwoods—
all the music his fingers danced
out of guitar and piano strings—
all the plants he grew
out of rocky Appalachian hills—
all the writing of others
he farmed in Ohio, his second home—

I pray he feels the love of families
gone ahead and left behind.
I stand in his broad circle of friends
hear his breath upon the land
and wait.

Old friend, I love you
like a brother.

And then…the word comes:
He is ashes now and I
cannot swallow it down.

My throat grips,
I cannot talk or write.

Last Words

His wife tells me
his last words were,
"Hold me," and
I cannot speak.
A breath falls between us.
I hold only the phone
and say, "He loved you so."

Through a glass darkly
I see his balded head
his deep eyes, broad smile,
a body grown frail
as the pale trillium.

His death is my mirror—
I taste my own absence
and miss my life, feel sorrow
for those I've loved for years.

She tells me when he
could no longer play the guitar
he sang softly till the end.

The blessing of his voice
and that my wife is near.

(5/28/2005)

Touching It

Day weary by late afternoon
I lie on my bed
in the darkness that surrounds.

Each breath
brings closer
this sense
of void
till I feel it
touching my skin
tangible and formed
and I name it—
emptiness.

I know it,
breathe it
into myself
taste how

emptiness is form
form, emptiness,
sense at last
its truth
beyond
hope or fear.

Five: The Cancer Poems, Living with It

Reading the Skies

A flock of starlings
moves together as one
with all the assurance
of a disease.
And my dog
does not look up
nor hide himself away
like a backyard dove.

My urologist calls:
I'm afraid your biopsy is positive.
Do you understand?
That means you do
in fact have cancer.
I swear I counted
my next twenty breaths
as the voice went on
explaining options I did
and did not have.

A cancer cell has random structure
and looks like blueberry pie.
Irregular and radical—
a death growth.
I close the book
know the biopsy was right
I've been marked like a tree
along an edge of green forest.

Again the starlings rise
from a nest of bushes;
and vanish into sky.
There are things
we can't remember.
I want this disease
to be one of those.

My dog pulls at the leash

and I look down at my feet,
step off the curb
move forward into space.

Shadows on the Water

That's how it feels, knowing
that your body carries cancer—
knowing that the shadow lies upon you,
sinks beneath your surface.

And you ask yourself again
how it entered and began.
What was it you did
that let it in?
And you try to image it,
a growth of cells that
feeds upon your health.

Alone on a bank you cast stones
through water and wait,
talk to your fears,
feel how always is near.
Who do you tell? Who do you
want to know so they can
remind you that your body
eats itself? Their advice,
a mirror of their lives.

I go out in the yard
and cut the grass knowing,
feeling my body sweat
as always, my back ache
with turning. What has changed—
only the knowing and the
still growth within.

I image it a lump
beneath the skin, knowing
I will never swim again with
the same ease for distance,
yet swim I will, close eyes
and plunge, water flowing about
and through me, hold onto

nothing, nothing I tell you.
Letting go, to go on
inside the light and shadow.

What You Realize When Cancer Comes

You will not live forever—No
you will not, for a ceiling of clouds
hovers in the sky.

You are not as brave
as you once thought.
Sounds of *death*
echo in your chest.

You feel the bite of pain,
the taste of it running
through you.

Following the telling to friends
comes a silence of
felt goodbyes. You come to know
the welling of tears.

Your children are stronger
than you thought and
closer to your skin.

The beauty of animals
birds on telephone lines,
dogs who look into your eyes,
all bring you peace.

You want no more confusion
than what already rises
in your head and heart.

You watch television less,
will never read all those books,
much less the ones
you have.

Songs can move you now, so that
you want to hold onto the words

like the hands of children.

Your own hands look good to you,
old and familiar
as water.

You read your lover's skin
like a road map
into yourself.

All touch is precious now.

There are echoes

in the words thrown
before you.

When they take your picture now
you wet your lips, swallow once
and truly smile.

Talk of your lost parents
pulls you out, and
brings you home again.

You are in a river
flowing in and through you.
Take a breath. Reach out your arms.
You can survive.

    A river is flowing
        flowing in and through you.
        Take a breath. Reach out your arms.

The Second Opinion

We go then, my wife and I, to the
Cleveland Clinic Cancer Center,
carrying films of my biopsy
under my arm. Each of us
taking a day off from work
to see what our future will be.
The building is a medical monument
planted along the edge of Hough,
Cleveland's black ghetto.
We park in the huge garage
walk the skywalk over dark streets,
the rain falling against the glass.
A steady traffic of families
seeking help. Each of us at the elevator
wondering who's dying, who's
going home. An elevator hush
lifting our secrecy to the right rooms.

On the tenth floor we get out
holding hands, entering the urology
waiting room, fifty or more couples
seated in rows of chairs looking out a
wall of windows on a city wet from misty sky,
above a grey-blue lake. "Heaven's
Waiting Room," I joke and sip a
hard swallow of water. Ann whispers,
"Take off your coat, we'll be here
for a while." She is right about so
many things, not just the medical
but the way it is dispersed...the record
keeping, the insurance checks, the
procedures and probes of intimacy.
Thirty years together, she has guarded me
from pain and death. Still she wonders
why I introduce her as "My wife, a
registered nurse." We smile from
time to time as couples rise and

walk off together into the rooms, cancer's
anniversary waltz, so sweet and sad
I do not speak of it to her.
Then we too shuffle off
down the hallway of charts and
equipment...meant to help save us.
And so we sit together
touch each other's hands, look out
again over earth below. My fear
of heights too slight to measure
against the dread inside my chest.
Why did I eat anything? My body
already full of this emptiness.
I pass a urine sample
into a coffee cup with my name.
I am probed by a young resident
"How's your continence?"
"Oh, and are you impotent?"
"No," I smile, my wife squeezing hard my hand,
both of us knowing last night's loving,
both of us knowing the 50-50 chance
it will survive a surgery. He reviews my
chart then asks me to remove my pants
to do a prostate check. Ann looks up,
"You can stay, honey," I say, bending over
for the pain to enter and leave quickly.
"No, I can't feel it," he says, and I am
left again with the mystery of this death wound
that only shows itself to a biopsy, to
technology's screen. I sigh and sit again
feeling the dread replaced by sadness
as I think of each of my children,
their soft faces tightened somehow
as I told them, their sweet words of
concern, "Dad, we love you, we need
to share this with you." Nothing medical
touches this for relief and comfort.

The door opens to a doctor in white
ten years my younger. He shakes

both of our hands and sits,
reviewing the charts, asking
the same questions, glancing
at one of my films against window light.
"You have a small prostate, Mr. Smith,"
as though it's a prize. "Yours is the
hardest case to advise. You're fifty-four,
with a low PSA score, a Gleason of only six.
Five years ago we never would have
detected this. We'd have caught it though
in your early sixties, when it would have spread
to the bone." He looks over at Ann,
back at me. We are both caught by this quick knowing.
And so we talk choices—radical surgery is clean,
conformed radiation not as radical, seed radiation
maybe cleaner still. And then the side effects
are listed with percentages...
incontinence...impotence...rectal damage...
Yet bottom line death is not spoken
but ever present, like the dark skies outside.
He rocks back and forward on his chair
as the words begin to cloud. He is
a black-jack dealer asking, "Okay,
do you want a hit? You already have 15 showing?
What will it be? The call is yours..."
We thank him, take back our films, his card,
walk down the hallway together,
get in our car and drive home,
clearer now in our uncertainty.

The Bone Scan

I enter the hospital as an "Outpatient,"
I don't belong here.
My doctor has sent me in for a bone scan;
they've found cancer in my prostate,
and want to establish "a base line."
I think for days on what this means...
some measure of how far along it is,
some measure of how long I have to go.
I dream about this, think on it over coffee.
(I'm to cut back on coffee...try green tea instead...
It's better for the prostate...
which I know now I am to lose.)

And so I am guided down a hallway,
told to wait outside "Nuclear Medicine."
The soft faces, thin ruffle of magazines...
A man comes with my file, "Larry...Smith."
I hear my name, therefore I am...alive.
Can't help these morose thoughts.
I have decided I must
pass this bone scan. So much
unexpected, bad news can wear you thin.
I must win at something, or I'm gone.
He has me sit, while he loads a needle
with radiation from a tube. "I'm going to
give you this in your left arm" and the
needle goes in.
"You may leave for three hours," he says,
"Drink lots of liquids, help the radiation to spread.
Return at one." *I hear, therefore I nod.*
"Yes, I'll be back at one."

I drive home thinking *I feel nothing, nothing.*
I sit around grading papers and watching an
old movie till almost one. I drive back,
find a place in the "Visitor's Parking" lot.
Across the street, I read the "Cancer Center" sign

realize for the first time, it is mine.
I cruise down the halls, and wait
till I have to urinate...powerful stuff
going down that drain. Again, "Larry...Smith"
and I rise on my own power,
enter a laboratory where I am to lie down.
"This is a very boring test," he says, "It lasts about
half an hour," guiding me with his eyes.
Only for me, this is not
boredom, this is life and death, this is
where I face my fate. A formula rises...
Prostate....10 years; Bone Cancer....maybe 2.
He has me lie on a plane, a padded board, with my
arms straight at my sides. A strap holds them there,
and I look down at my feet so distant
in the tube that will cover me.
I can get through this, looking at the ceiling tile.
He sits at his computer, starts the machine, a low hum
to fill the room. I close my eyes, try to count my breath...
Cannot, cannot slow it to count, as though the engine hum
pulls me too. I try again and again to rest,
almost there, I open my eyes to the white wall of it...
pressed an inch from my face. *So close, so close.*
Can I get through this?
                                    And then a strange thing,
I begin to feel comforted by this machine, as it moves
so carefully along my body, a millimeter at a time.
I think of my wife's warm hands doing touch therapy
running over my body, a shaman pulling me through.
I close my eyes again, and begin to breathe in time.
For half and hour, I am watched over
by this loving machine. I look over at my guide,
watching his computer screen. My body
a tiny skeleton...front and back. What do those
bright areas mean? And again, the slow dance
of the machine over me. "This is almost
like Reiki, or touch therapy," I tell him. He nods
and looks away. "Don't speak."

And I don't speak or move or do anything but

breathe and think, hear my heart still beating,
until I'm told to rise. "That's it. You can put on
your shirt and shoes, your belt."
It is then I think to ask...*How much does he know?*
How much has his machine already told him?
He is handing me a form and I dare to ask,
"So, how does it look? Can you tell anything?"
There is a long and painful pause. "Who's your doctor?"
I tell him, and he looks down at the forms.
"He should know by Monday. Give him a call then."
I drink what this could mean, another form
of cancer, this knowing and not.
"Okay, I will," I say, "Should I do anything
for the radiation?" He opens the door, "No.
The radiation will dissolve into your bones."
I walk down the hallway moving towards home.

Resting

My daughter stretches out beside me
on her college bed, and whispers,
"How are you doing?" I tell her
how the cancer grows
in circles of dread, how I
deal with it in waves
of confrontation and fear.
The bone scan waiting,
the waking up to it each day.
She puts her head against my chest
and we breathe softly,
feel my old heart rest.

(Athens, Ohio, 9/28/97)

Visiting the Cleveland Museum of Natural History

Today we drive the long hour
into Cleveland, across that bridge,
past the stacks and towers, along
a blue-white lake, up Rockefeller Park
to the museums near the Circle.
My daughter and her husband sit quiet
in the backseat while their new baby sleeps.

It is too early, so we go instead
to the Arabica Café for coffees
and scones, talk of what we've
done all week, hear the buzz of
other people's words. Then I see
students reading in corners,
think of papers I have to grade,
check my watch, and say, "Time
to move along."

In the museum parking lot: November leaves
covered with a new snow, dark starlings
perched in bare boughs. We go in,
hang our coats, begin to share our walk...
So much here seems the same—dry bones
and feathers, Indian tools and headdresses,
animals and art united, humans held to scale.
At the replica of the Adena burial mound
I pause at the glass, hear the silence deep inside.

As I push the baby's stroller
into the dinosaur room suddenly
she emits a squeal—a cry
beyond the call of birds—
waking me from my native sleep.
I feel the life of wings and flesh
of wind and sea and sky.
My own hearts stirs, sharp breath
to speak the life that's left,
turn bones to flutes and charms.

Later seated on a bench, my eyes and voice too full,
I tell my wife, "My brain feels atrophied,"
She strokes my arms and smiles,
"It will come back to you."

I sit on the wooden bench
touch my hands to my face
and wait.

Telling an Old Friend

For Zita

I sit in the small town café
with an old friend and tell her
my cancer story—how they found it,
what's been done, what choices are left to me—
and she does not interrupt with advice
or stories about other friends. Instead
she nods and listens while I play this
strange-sad music across our table
above our glasses of water, our
empty coffee cups. And when the
waitress finally comes, we turn our
minds to choices of eggs and toasts,
decaf or regular. It is that pause
between songs on a record or tape,
and we're both wishing the new song
will lift us above the mortality of
words to visions and connections shared.

She begins telling me the story
or her sixtieth birthday, spent
among the Rockies. They had
reached the highest point
above the clouds and gotten out
of their car. "Go on," Paul said,
"I can't breathe so high," and she,
afraid of heights, had climbed the
last few yards to the peak, "I looked out...
and knew that this was it—the top—
below was snow, and below that the
clustered towns with streets and cars."
It is I now who listens and waits
as she smiles softly, "I'd spent my life climbing
and could see now what was left to me."
"I know," I say, gesturing toward the wall,
"I can sense now the way things
begin and end."

We drink our coffees and spread
jellies on our breads. I tell of a
book I've finished, she of an exhibition
of her art. It is food enough
until we rise, hold each other close
there in the late breakfast hour,
then walk out together into light.

The Lightning

My wife rolls over and says, "I think the furnace is dead." I go on reading in bed beside her.

I turn the lamp out and take off my glasses, lay them on the floor under the bed.

An hour goes by while I think about things...the cost of a new furnace, where the kids are in their lives, the sound of the wind, the wind....

In my dream I am softly descending the stairs, carrying a candle down to the furnace. There is no sound or smell, as I bend over to look into its face. I do not like this furnace. It is not my friend but an old man who watches wordlessly. I bring the candle up to see inside....a huge roar, then all is darkness...all is gone.

I wake up shaking, struggling for air, see the nightlight through the darkness and try to lay still without waking Ann. I think of my father, a furnace man, who died suddenly while I was away. What would he say to me now? What have I to say to him?

My legs are feeling cold now, so I sit up, gather my glasses and walk into the hall. The thermostat is set at 70 degrees. The temperature is 58. I must go down.

From the cupboard I take a flashlight and descend the cellar stairs...their creaking in the night, the dog's nails clicking down the steps behind me.

There is the furnace cold and silent. I bend to look inside, see the pilot light is out. I turn the gas off and on again, smell the death it can bring.

I hold down the button, counting. Make each breath my first and last. Then reach down and light the match.

The Massage

for Laura

In the back room
of their bungalow
a massage table
two dressers—one of wood,
the other wicker;
on one oils,
the other an altar
of gauzy scarf and
pictures of Issa.
Through the curtains
a frozen yard,
inside the soft music
of summer jazz,
thin aroma of incense sticks.
I fold my shirt
upon the chair
stretch out beneath
the flannel sheet.
Her baby with her husband
sleeping now in the other room.
She enters smiling
begins to work my back
a daughter's hands
small and strong
reach inside my old shell
untie the knots.

In the Fish Tank

All day the black molly
has hung around the top
of the bowl, floating aimless,
at times flicking its long tail—Not yet.
Each time I enter the room
I look over at him—water
bubbling around his dark body.
Remembering my dad's old trick
I salt the water lightly
watch it dissolve...
He flicks his tail, then rises
unable to get any depth,
lost stones shine
a fathom below.
Outside the window are branches,
bare bones in winter light.
The radio plays old Christmas songs.
To pick up a book,
to write across a page...
None of it feels right like a
Sunday walk through woods.
I look over at the fish, still moving;
I lie back and
close my eyes.

Walking Through

We wake before the sun arrives,
before her mother starts coffee
on her kitchen stove.
Back in our old town
we are guests at home
my wife and I, the woman
I first kissed inside
this kitchen door. "Ready?"
She asks and we are gone
dressed in winter warm.
We pass beyond the houses
climbing the steep hills
dusted now with snow.
The roar of the mill fades
like a radio station.
Walking in our fifties
to keep alive, pump cool air
into our lungs, oxygen high.

Yes, this walking has a destination
a point on our trail.
Trading stories we go up, then down:
an abandoned house through trees,
a yellowed mining stream beside the road...
Finally we climb through grass and gate
to the cemetery grounds
and my parents' graves.
Alone among neighbors' names
they lie in peaceful air.
"Look," my wife calls—a moon
through trees here—a sun under clouds there.
Standing over them in a fresh fog
touching everything
I have no words.
"Delbert and Jean Smith," I read aloud
and begin raking with my hands
the leaves and weeds
clustered at the marker's foot.

A cold damp soils my skin
and I am breathing hard
the weight of emotion held too long.
No bird calls, only wind...
Suddenly my wife hugs my back
and we lean together there, so that
I cannot speak aloud the greeting
I would bring, but think it hard
into the ground, "Mother, Father—
I am coming towards you...
Slowly towards you..."
Only my wife's arms warm me
till we walk back into the life
of this old and noisy town.

The Testing in Seattle

I.
I stare down at my feet
on the pale bathroom tile
of the Hospital Inn.
Letting the enema
work through me
we begin again
the round of tests
that will take my prostate
from me, an organ
drawn like a heart
on the page,
shrink it to a peach pit
ready to discard, forgetting
the three children
it helped bring,
the miracle nights
of warm loving
sweet enterings.
Gone bad now, breeding death cells,
to be vanished with radiation seeds.
I'm not to approach pregnant women
or hold babies on my lap...Outside
I hear the Seattle sirens
as the sun comes on under clouds.
Across the way, hospital rooms
stand half lit as the day crew
comes on in new scrubs:
entering rooms, waking people
with soft sips of water
pulling them gently
back into day.

II.
At the Cancer Center
I find my place
seated among older men

my father's age, now mine.
All of us knowing what lies within.
All of us wanting to begin again
reborn from radiation seeds.
One fellow tells of his Nebraska farm;
another asks how soy beans grow,
and none of us speak of the cancer,
holding truth and our bladders
till the post-exam.
The receptionist speaks too loud
on the phone with a man from Des Moines,
"You're having complications...can't urinate?"
Someone asks the farmer, "How much land
do you own?" Proud in his blue cap:
"800 acres, I reckon. I irrigate."
Silence and nods, "Say," he adds,
"We all come here 'cause these folks
are the best at their field...right?"
"Sure," I smile into his broad acre face,
"We're all taking our best chance."
He grins big, "I don't want no surgeon
working me over, or no rookie. Don't want to be a
guinea pig and end up dead." Silence
fills the room with his twice-declared truth.
We sit quiet in the little room, cancer comrades
without the knife.

III.
A nurse named Sally walks me
down the hall into the room, asks me
the weather in Ohio, smiles and tells me,
"Remove your clothes beneath the waist.
Then climb up on the table. You can
cover yourself with the sheet till I return."
A small sadness floats through the room
as I stare down at my feet,
lie back and lift my legs
into the irony of stirrups.
When she enters again, she
dims the lights and gently

probes inside me. I slow my breath,
watched over as I am
by machines.

IV.

When the doctor enters I rise
to shake his hand, say his name,
an homage to the gods, knowing
I will have but fifteen minutes
to speak my fate. I listen
as he speaks softly of
options and percentages, try to
read meaning from numbers into years.
Outside his windows, clouds pass
slowly through towers. Inside my pocket
my thumb runs over the smooth bone
of seagull that I found on my Ohio beach,
an amulet against all death. For a moment
I hear just our tones, feel his deference
to my life, mine to his skills.
In three months it will be over
and I can live again
until I don't.

V.

Walking back through rain
I enter my hotel room
empty in late afternoon.
I lie down upon the bed
and cannot call home
not yet until I shower, water running
off my stooped back.
And in the mirror at last
I recognize my pain
hold the towel
long against my face.
Across the way a young man
sits in soft light listening to someone
propped up in a bed. I

brush back my hair
sit with towel in chair
and call my love
hear my life
wed to hers
once more.

The Writing

"But I want to get up early one more morning, at least.
And go to my place with some coffee and wait.
Just wait, to see what's going to happen."
—Raymond Carver, "At Least"

I've been reading the tribute, *Remembering Ray*,
for Raymond Carver, lost to lung cancer
a decade now, and each piece has that
deep connection, standing down,
feet on the ground. His writing too
had that close watching for movement,
clear listening into words;
he held and gave back hard truths
inside the facts. I can't help thinking
of his wife Tess, riding out those
last days with him, taking the calls
and letters from friends, living the long grief
that enters our lives. Ray would have
written it all into a story, "The Writer's Wife,"
entering the life and language still and transparent,
taking everything on its own terms,
spilling over the empty fullness
of our bright and shadowed days:
a breath, a word, a page, a story
completed at last.

Thinking of You in Seattle

For Denise and Laura

I walk the wet streets,
duck inside a corner café
for a scone and cup
of Earl Grey. People
walk across the street
past my windowed table
carrying their bodies and faces
through morning rain.

In *Seattle Weekly* I read again
of the death of Denise Levertov
a poet whose light so freely
fell upon the world—
touching and tasting everything
breaking silence tenderly.
Her photo is newsprint soft—
eyes that know, a smile that shares
our joy and pain. And I
touch it lightly as she
once touched my cheek. "Thank you,"
I said, "for all your acts and words.
You taught me how to care."
She heard only my eyes
and blessed me with a kiss
that felt like a poem.
I fold the paper gently now
into my bag, take it home
to my daughter in Ohio
who turns her own words
into prayers.

Working Around It

All day I have been carrying deep messages
to myself. The bank machine this morning
tells me "You have insufficient funds,"
and I drive off towards school. My office
answering machine flashes, then speaks,
"We regret to inform you that your request
for health care coverage outside the network
has been denied." *It doesn't matter,*
I want to say aloud but know it is my life
being talked about. I let my head rest
on my hands and try to breathe clean—
This news that kicks your gut.
I have a class to teach
in five minutes.

At home I am grading papers
when I hear a crash. "Ann?" I yell,
"Are you alright?" Nothing, then
"Ann?" I rise with the fear... "Honey...
are you okay!" I think heart attack
as I step into the room, see her standing
at the closet door, "What? I couldn't
hear you," she smiles back into
my bewildered face turning from fear
to anger then love, "I was afraid
something happened to you. I was afraid
that you were hurt."

Later we pick up our daughter's family
and go to grocery shop. On the drive I
am silent as they sing to the radio, yet each bass note
echoes in my heart. I park the car as they go in.
I am lost till I find Laura and Rosa by the bananas,
"Where's your mother?" I ask. "In the restroom.
She said to go ahead, she'd catch up."
Again I feel alone, even as her husband joins us.
We shop and talk and Ann comes up
by the wine and tea. "We missed you,"

I smile above the water.

It is not until the Mexican restaurant
where the baby fusses so that the waiter
forgets our order and brings water instead.
It is not until then that I take the baby
onto my lap, holding her softly in my arms, that she
turns quick bumping her head on the table edge.
It is then I stare into her face, watch real hurt
rise into her eyes, spread across her lips,
tears coming to her cheeks.
And my own pain suffocates my chest,
till I want to cry with her—*I want no one*
to suffer and be denied. I begin to break down
in this little Mexican restaurant with its
dark faces watching me. But then the waiter
brings our food, and I sit back.
"Be careful, please. It's very hot—the plate."
I drink water and swallow food.

That night, I pull the covers up around my neck,
take what comfort the bed gives, try not to think,
as my wife turns to my face, her arms warm
beneath the sheets, reaching to me, her eyes
clear and deep, "What's been hurting you?"
I cannot speak nor want to hide, as we
hold each other safe in the night,
for slowly, slowly the rock within my chest
begins to break and water flows outside.
We rock together there in our cradle of arms,
and I reach the other side of knowing
where I survive without making friends of this cancer,
but allow its pain to flow through me like water.

Gathering

"Make of yourself a light."
(Buddha's last words)

I.

The night before we fly to Seattle
Ann and I stay with her brother,
wife, and baby. The talk is light,
the food comfortable and spiced
with words of family, and then
we sleep in their guest bed, too high
and hard for making love. Next day
we only speak of my surgery as we
hug them goodbye...
May you be well.

Airports like shopping malls, flood with people
walking off—sitting and waiting in lines—
disappearing down long hallways, as we do now.
At the window seat, I look out to Ohio rain,
then try to breathe slow, say soft words
of letting go . . . *May I be well.*
May I be kind. May I be free.
We taxi out, then rise through clouds,
falling asleep as we glide.

II.

Shuttled to old Seattle hotel
we nest in room across from hospital.
May they be cared for.
May they be well.
Ann showers, I bathe, and we
each stretch out in twin beds.
Talk is of tomorrow's schedule,
today's medication. While she naps
I listen to John Denver sing of
"Poems and Prayers and Promises";
his old gone voice turns inside me now.
Yesterday I phoned the clinic to be sure
the operation was scheduled.
Now on Seattle hotel bed

for a moment I say to myself, *No,*
This is wrong. We will go home now.
Then wait a long moment—enough to feel
the choice to stay is right and mine.
I watch Ann sleep softly and read more
of Jack Kornfield's *A Path With Heart,*
a song of opening...
May I be filled with loving-kindness...
May I be peaceful and at ease.
To which I add...
May I accept this cancer, allow it
to flow through me.

Before it all begins, we walk wet Seattle streets.
While Ann buys incense and essential oils,
I pick up a birth stone card marked "Cancer,"
drawn to it as my name—I touch this piece
of soap stone—as my own.

The hospital doors glide open to the Pre-Admit,
where I complete forms, am guided back to a little room,
lie upon a table as pads and machine
extract the map of my heart.
Across the room Ann's smile leads me.
A guy comes. "I'm one of the blood men,"
and he takes a sample from my vein,
Soon the nurse returns to say, "Everything
looks good for tomorrow."

Back in our hotel room I lie on the little bed
write haiku in my mind...

    Beyond the curtains
    are the many windows of
    the hospital rooms.

We make love that evening as though
it might be our last. Entering and
holding her close into the night.

III.
We wake hours before the operation,
lie in our separate beds, reading
and talking the clock around. Finally
Ann lights a candle and incense stick,
"Let's do therapeutic touch." No need to ask
as I lay down my book, stretch out beneath
her sheet. Slowly she moves energies around,
hers and mine in gentle balancing—
    Form is exactly emptiness.
    Emptiness is exactly form.

At the main entrance again
I am skirted off to the left.
Everyone is so polite to us, giving calm
assurance to the day—
    May you be well...
    May you be happy...
I have brought with me small copies
of Lao Tzu's *Tao Te-Ching* and *Nature Poems*
edited by my daughter. That day I read
only a poem from each, yet know
they are there for me, even as I sit
inside the silence of candlelight
in the hospital chapel.

IV.
We are ushered back to our "pod,"
a big chair and curtains, a closet
for the clothes I disrobe...wallet, watch...
only their bracelet to name me now.
I put on the pajamas of treatment
soft slippers to scoot along
following the anesthesiologist
into the operating room. . . Ann is gone
swept away like my robe and pants,
as I climb aboard the table
where I am clothed in a warm white sheet.
At my ear the soft voice of the anesthesiologist
explains what's to be done—a spinal and

enough to guide me through.
The lights are dim—equipment held in shadow.
He starts my IV, rubs a cold local for the spinal.
So quiet here, as my doctors
come through the door, smiling
and I agree to everything—
Let it begin.

Into soft stirrups my legs are lifted
beyond me now as I drift through deep quiet—
other doctors masked—talking—calling numbers:
"Six?"—"Yes, six."—"Perfect"—"Six again?"
"Yes, six."—"Perfect."—"Six again?" . . .
It goes beyond my counting as I float
inside its rhythm, feeling nothing,
thinking only, *Thus . . . Thus . . . Thus . . .*
And then both doctors come around
saying, "Well, it went just fine. Looks
very good." One shows me a screen,
"This is your urethra." I look down,
see pulsing flesh from within,
yet what pulls me more is another screen,
silver gray of prostate ultrasound—
vast Milky Way cloud of tiny black stars:
each radiation seed inside me now—
constellation of healing.
Not reverse of birth, for I will nurture
these within my flesh till they dissolve,
break away dead soil,
do their work.

Ann's face is smiling over mine—
above are ceiling tile, a painted sea
we have come through together.
And so we wait for feeling to return—
the long story of this cancer—an awakening
to what lies within, how long and close
we hold on...how care and compassion
flood the heart to overfull.

This Is a Poem About

Waiting and not knowing while
things are happening around you.

Thinking of how you were well
before the operation, and now
you are not, how the sting of
radiation seeds swells your groin
with the birth of something.

Telling people you're doing okay
but can't make it to their house
when they think you should be well
now that you've been treated.

Feeling confusion in the middle of
sentences, thoughts draining out
blurred to gray with medication
and uncertainty.

Hurrying to the bathroom and
watching for blood in your urine,
trying to relax enough to pee
into the bowl.

Lying beside your wife, afraid
to touch her warm back,
afraid of what might and
might not come of it.

Swallowing the pills again and again
trying to make friends of them
losing count.

Wanting to believe that
what grows in you
is health
when it feels most
like a cancer.

Recovering

I lie in bed resting in mid-afternoon.
The wind is puffing back the curtains
and I wonder if these seeds inside me
are doing their work, turning my prostate
into a harmless gland again. Am I
cancer free and what will that mean?

Hope sweetens my days and allows me
to forget what might yet loom inside.
For now I suffer the immediate pain
of my organs of elimination.
The "discomfort" the doctors spoke of
casually in their high office
lives inside me now—sharp burn
of urination as though I'm passing
a radiation stone, the rising soreness
in my groin and rectum, hurt reminders.

And yet life goes on, except for the
rushing to the bathroom, the
dumb waiting while the urine
drips out, the stress around
sexual intimacy, causing me to
feel the erections of my dreams,
reach down to know it can
happen again...wondering and knowing
the cost of fear and pain
between us now. Awaiting a time when
all this will be a memory
soon.

Living with It

I live with a different fear now,
that I might get well
enough to die again
some other way.
It makes no sense and
yet it does.
I had crossed the bridge over cancer
accepted its flow through me
and now I face the blank cold
of the unknown. Of course I know
the freedom this new cure brings,
the release to play again. Of course I
want to read the faces of my children
forever and forever, yet know now
how each cycle has its end.
The faces of flowers open to it.
The trees release their leaves to it.
I have labored in rain and shadow
to realize this, to claim its truth
upon my skin. And now I know
I must do so again.

Recognition

Wednesday we rise early.
And while Ann dresses,
packs her bags, I make coffee,
read the paper. The dog fussing lightly
at my feet fearing he will be left behind

On the way to the airport we talk
haltingly. She is already there,
a thousand miles away,
yet turns to say, "Oh, Dr. Bob called…
He wants to start a men with cancer
support group." I nod, okay,
look out to fields stretched to trees
under a thin layer of clouds.

At the airport she checks in
while I park the car. Walking
down the concourse she stops,
to say, "You don't have to wait with me."
And I, "This is where I want to be."
Before she boards we kiss, say our love
quiet in the crowd.

   Walking out
I pass a tall thin man
in khaki pants, blue short sleeve shirt,
so familiar, with three kids at his side.
And then I feel it, a welling in my throat
that breaks inside the tears.
That man is me, thirty years ago.
This that I am here now is me.
So who do I mean these tears for?
Who is it I mourn?

Driving home I pass the fields
of wheat, sagging gently
under a thin cover of rain.

Before the Sun

*"Every brush stroke was a living thing;
one movement of the arm could create a whole world."*
                    -Gretel Ehrlich

The train that crosses town
dashes through my heart
pounding its way to market
shaking the ground I stand upon.
And I taste the fear and sadness
of passing life. *Should I be somewhere
doing something now?*
At fifty-five I wait and wonder.
Is this train leaving me behind?
Worry drives my mind
while I stand impatient on the walk
sidetracked before the gate asking,
Where am I going—where have I been?

Paused so until the words on boxcars
blur before me so I feel my
breath break open into sun.
Outside the rush and rumble—
a silken flow of breath release.

I turn aside to weeds beside the tracks—
bright and greeny stems of chicory
resilient and humble flowers
growing blue and tender
washed in sun.

Leaning Together in a Storm

Twelve older men in shirt sleeves
sit around the Cancer Center
sipping ice water and making jokes
waiting for the meeting to begin.
"Ever notice how no one parks
in the Cancer Center zone?"
I am one of them tonight
meant to acknowledge
our story within
our private brotherhood.

The counselor rises to welcome us
asks each to state his cancer story:
give his name and dates
the procedure we chose
tell how long he's survived.
And I take real joy
in hearing them speak
sensing their eyes, their bodies
seated beside me here.

Then a door opens
and our leader rises
to introduce the night's speaker
a young surgeon, his slide-tray at his side.
"Greetings, Gentlemen," he grins
snapping on his slides, projecting
our organs onto the wall,
touching them with his pointer
in blunt precision,
warning us again of lymph nodes
cells outside the prostate
that can end our life.
We swallow a hundred nightmares
with smiles and nods.

I interrupt his gay delivery,
"What about orgasm...?"

"Forget orgasm," he grins,
"You don't have a prostate."
Another asks about second opinions,
"Go ahead...what can it hurt?" then adds,
"Unfortunately it won't help much either."
I want to escape this torture by words,
but ask instead, "And what about the
radiation seed implants they're doing in Seattle?"
He turns on me like a cop. "We're doing those now.
So it's a question, how big is your ego?"
Some smile at this, others know
how cold the knife is, how his words
cut across our lives, our wish to live
each breath, see morning spread
across our lawn, our grandchildren's faces.
We all have this unspoken need
to pace our life
like a heart beat.

In the end we let it go
trade our feelings for facts
we already know,
"It's a game of numbers,"
he says again, and I wonder
if these others want to drive
this witch doctor from the room
and gather warmth from the fire
we sit around, share our stories
together of going on

Man to Man

For Bob Daniels and the guys

Two urologists in suits
come in from Cleveland
to talk to our cancer group.
The lights go dim,
and in charts and graphs
they dispense their facts
as if we were surgeons
with our prostates in tact.

But we are not. We have
each already gone under knife,
radiation beam or seed.
This is old history to us,
but we listen, wait, and wonder.
And when someone asks them
to predict our futures,
their faces grow glum
and darken with doubt.
"To be honest," the younger says,
"We're not sure, in the long run,
if any of this really works,
if any of it stops the real
metastasis or cancer growth."
An empty silence creeps around us
as they go on, these troubled priests
who disturb our faith
rob us of our own special truth.

The lights come on,
the chatter starts,
cookies are passed,
but no one dares to touch again
the essential dark.

(May 2000)

What Is Needed

I scan the paper
for the morning's news,
numb myself
to distant bombings
crimes of power
the abuse we daily give
each other. I let them
enter my mind yet I
block my heart—
items on a menu card
I pass over.

But then
there is this photo—
a young boy dying
from leukemia in a
hospital bed, lying
on his side, his small
pajamaed arm resting
outside the covers
almost asleep. And it
touches me so, this
unspoken song of
going on, of living
through each small breath.

I want to lay my head
beside his soft cheek
whisper *you are loved forever*
help him keep
the child alive.

The Turnings

One

I am sitting in my car
at the Rye Beach intersection
watching two people
quarrel in the car before me.
They are fighting with words
and looks, their cigarettes
pointing at the other's face
in mute pantomime, like a
scene from a Raymond Carver story.
The light changes, they make their turn,
a loose exhaust pipe spews angry smoke
into wintry air.

Two

At the movies, I sit alone
waiting my wife's return
from the restroom,
watching couples stroll in
choosing their seats together,
and I feel divorced from
company, waiting for the
lights to dim, the trailers
to begin. As I stare out
I notice a simple thing—
the way lovers' heads
turn to each other
in a kind of glow, while others talk
as they stare ahead as if watching
traffic or television or the distant horizon
together and alone. The lights dim,
the music begins and I
search again
for my lover's eyes.

Three

At the cancer support group
husbands and wives
sit in a close circle.
Women with breast cancer,
men with their prostates removed,
together with their mates this time.
I take a cookie, cup of decaf
and sit among them.
Outside the meeting room
a janitor looks in. He is
doing his job, gathering trash
from the hospital rooms.
We are welcomed, the lights are dimmed
and a videotape begins—"Dealing
with Your Diagnosis." We know these people
as our friends. We drink in the dark,
hear their words as our own. The lights
come on. "Reactions?" Dr. Bob begins.
Only the sound of voices across
the partition...and then a woman's voice
releases itself into the room, telling
the story of the road they've been on
recounting the blocks and setbacks,
the ways of family and friends.
Tears rise in the husband's eyes.
It is his cancer and their pain.
He looks up from his shoes
over at her face, the one
that has been loving him
for such a long time.
I set my Styrofoam cup
down on the table
speak into the silence—
"I see this all as a river—the cancer
coming to me, gliding in and through me,
a flow to guide me, even here
and now." Quiet. Breath.

In confessing pain
I feel release, turn to feel
my wife's warm hand.

Cancer Check-Up

My cancer test says
maybe nothing—maybe
the growth goes on.

My car stops dead on Crocker Road,
and I pull off, sit there quiet,
shaking with tears.

My computer crashes and I feel
I will be dying soon.

The car gets a jump
and a new alternator;
the computer
a new hard drive.

There are no transplants for cancer,
no blankets to hide under,
no place to spit the dread.

In the morning's mirror—
my life's face—still there,
still learning to live
by letting go.

Cancer Note

Do not send cash, cash equivalent,
    or jewelry.
Do not send lies and pity, advice
    or regrets.
Do not send your fears and worries
    onto mine.
We all deal with this in our own
    manner and time.
We all find our own space
    to move from.
I grieve with you the loss
    of those you've loved.
The faces of children rise up
    in our bread.
We all will die someday,
    but till then...
Send your concern and wishes only
    and listen with me
Our hearts are beating still.

Six: Traveling, Taking Leave at Daybreak

Calligraphy of Birds

Hundreds of starlings
stream across the sky,
their bodies turning colors
in the setting sun.

And I stand on the street
reading their flight
as my dog pulls his leash.
Their chatter among trees
then small bodies rising
to sweep the sky and vanish.

What holds me so
while neighbors rake yards
and cars honk their horns?

In my sixth decade
my own path erases—
leaves swept by wind
into the lake.
Twin comfort of something larger
and not leaving a trace.

(3/6/2004)

Canoeing in Mid-October

Three sleek canoes
    gliding along
            through what comes:
            my daughter and her husband
        my son, his wife and son
my wife and myself—
fall leaves overhead
    and below the water's
            shimmering face.
            Our oars stroke
        down and through
in teams of two.
The air is cool and clear
    the water cold and deep
            rippling under us.
            We have dressed
        in layers, life jackets
in case we tip.

My son helped plan this trip
    my wife and daughter make it flow
            their spouses paddle and steer.
            My father and mother
        watch from above as we
glide in long slim canoes
over rocks and rapids
    past old camping trailers
            like theirs once.
            The river's sounds
        hold our quiet
journeying home.
We go over the rough spots
    turning in time to watch
            the others make it through.
            Have we taught them anything?
        Have they learned the
ways of going on?

A great blue heron rises
    from bush through leaves to sky
            flapping its long grey wings.
            My grandson calls and reaches
        down through waters as
his father steadies the boat.
In my son's smiling face
    I see my father, his son,
            and I there too.
            Do these others know
        the quiet joy
they bring me?

Three canoes
    gliding along
            through what comes
            giving my heart
        the courage to see
only two.

Sheldon's Marsh in Mid-Summer:
"A Bird's Wing Sweeps the Sky"

A row of turtles lie sunning
on a log in the still pond
between the lush marsh trees
and the golf course green.
Wood thrush echo themselves
above the distant rumble of a train.

I sit on the rough boards
of the lookout, my cell phone
left in the car.

And I do not open the book
of poems, read instead the sunlight
moving slowly across marsh grass,
rich smells of the bog, soft croaking of frogs.
Just above the telephone lines
a row of geese glide in to land
not like in the movies, but
like themselves here and now,
wordless in afternoon wind—
a feather on the ground.

(8/1/2003)

Walking the Castalia Quarries

When I walk the quarry rim with its
lush locust trees and sun drenched butterflies,
I think how strange beauty can be
here where earth's been dug and turned again.

Go slow to see the insects in the grass,
the blue-white moths that land on your hat brim.
The pond along the ledge—oasis if there ever was—
water spiders dancing, fossils etched in limestone.

Wood thrush deep in bushes, song cascading
like the vines through branches. Smell of cinnamon.
Turkey vultures glide on thermals near power lines
where you turn, begin the slow descent to find again.

The wooden bench with her name: *Molly Stewart...*
frail girl-woman who sketched this place
in delicate lines, tender shadings to speak its beauty.
Brushing back her hair, her eyes
already dying while she lived,
touching such wildness to her skin
loving it enough to make it last.

Taking Leave at Daybreak

Rising in the dark I gather clothes
taking my first journey's step
over the sleeping dog—
breaking the silence with a shower.

My wife in pink pajamas makes coffee,
retreats to covers while I dress for travel
tonight to undress in another city
by the light of a hotel television.

Slippery on the walk newly frosted
I carry my bags into the colors of dawn.
A neighbor out walking turns and nods
as I close the trunk.

At the window my wife stands smiling,
the dog is ready to be fed.
All day we will taste each other's absence.
Wild geese are calling overhead.

Gliding

In a plane I am always drawn
to the earth below, always choose
the windowed seat, read the landscape
below, the way tufts of trees
shape the earth, lines that
rise and fall, the rivers
of margins, houses in pebbled
clusters and rows.
                              I drift
out the window, glide off the wing
in a gentle speed that breathes
over everything. Flying thus
I know my life is more
than books and talk
more than regret and intent.
This soft unspoken sunlight
deepens textures like a hand
extended from childhood—one
I fly over and through
a thousand times.

Magee Marsh in Early Spring

The trees stand bare in wind
as clouds move across the sun,
yet inside the glade, birds sing.
Canadian geese stroll the bank
followed by cackling goslings;
Wild ducks call across the bay
as the wind awakens listening.

    A great blue heron glides
    across the road setting down
    its fragile legs and feet
    upon the crest of grass,
    its deep plumed robe folding.

    Along a stream a great white egret
    spreads its breeding plumes
    soft crested invitation
    to the morning.

I let my binoculars hang upon my chest
I let the landscape be my thoughts
and breathe by available light.

Sheldon's Marsh

We walk out through spring woods
into the deep and clear of morning—robins
warbling on the sycamore, a red-tailed hawk
gliding over the tall maples. My son and I
stopping to follow the call of a black throated warbler,
our wives strolling ahead through talking leaves.
The marsh water is high this year and we
do not hear the splash and sludge of summer carp.

At the lookout point our wives walk on
and we step out onto the wooded deck,
listen for birds in wind. He looks down,
searches the wild grass while I lift binoculars
survey the bay for heron and swan.
A few geese glide overhead, some circling gulls, and then
 this thin line of great white egret
circling the marsh lagoon—each at its lookout post,
each as still as snow, as obvious as white.
I watch a long time till slowly an egret
rises from his pod, stretches wings like flapping sheets,
and lifts into the light. Its long and tender neck curves
inward for flight. It glides—it glides—
lands on the branch of another who rises—
glides and glides to a further rock where another
rises in a rite grown deeper for the light.
I try to speak this to my son, but he
stares into a brood of grass—there, he says
a black mole inside the grass. He is right.
We watch it move among the shadows,
and I do not ask him again to read my egret.

We stand and wait for our wives. The wind sings
through huge willows. My wife walks over
to me, and his to him. We tell of mole
and egret, they of the peace of turtles.
We follow back the path without words,
all of us knowing we have survived.

Ohio October, Route 4

*"Nature in wildest extravagance held her structure
as common as gravel-piles."*

John Muir

Today the way the grass looks
is enough, how the sun comes up
slow behind me as I drive
past fields of tanning corn
lit by a red tasseled glow that
points to a blue breath of sky.
I swear the colors ripen
as the light rises and spreads
across a gold-green field
of soybean plants resting
from harvest. And suddenly
a field of yellow suns stemmed to earth
gives eyes the chance to see
close growth. Impossible to say
how these lines of crops
meet each other so, rounding shapes,
holding ground, giving forth, making
today seem always and near.

Polishing a Stone

My back lies on the smooth boards
of a redwood deck by the marsh.
Already the cattails turn soft
as my sweater bunched under my head.
No music here but the call of geese
crossing under a pale blue sky.
The sun comes out and I close my eyes;
the shade tells me when to open again.
There is so little to say really.
We journey out and return again.
Tonight we will cook wild rice, and eat it
with vegetables from our garden.

In the Middle of Rye Beach Road

I stop behind the blue Ford pickup
behind the red mini-van,
before the railroad crossing
on the road to work.
A Conrail train glides by
shuffling freight cars to Chicago.
Above the trees, only sun.
Below, horses running in a field.

And I look down the middle strip
to an animal dead in the road.
Its fur alive in the light tells me
it is freshly dead, recently alive.
I pause a long moment
think about the train, the traffic,
how much time has gone by
how much is left...Can I
wait this out? I sit back, look away
to fields of young soybean plants.

No, I am getting out, walking
up the middle, to the small body
spread out like a stuffed animal,
its legs stretched out at last—
A rabbit at my feet, its small head
crushed by wheels going too fast to slow.
I bend down, take its legs
in my hand, and toss lightly its soft body
into the tall green weeds.

Walking back I do not look
at the faces of the others;
I have been them, alone in my car.
Just now, pulled out and into this moment
I breathe hard and pray
it will somehow be enough.

In Early Spring

Road catkins, russet and tan, let the
wind sweep over them as dusk
seeps in along the lake,
and I pass road puddles
swelling to ponds, mirroring
the sky's own silveriness.
At the railroad tracks seven geese
veer off and set down in a field
so that only their necks
speak for them, telling us all
to go on while they rest
by the barn. Today a man
asked me if I were depressed,
and I looked up and smiled.
No more than these geese or catkins
as lights falls around them, no
more than those pine boughs
lifting in the wind—just so,
life goes on.

Walking Through Woods in Early Spring

Grasses bury the trail edge through trees.
My son chases after his son
running three-year-old legs down the path
as he passes rare trillium along the bank—
watches a black butterfly in tall grass—
follows a wooden footbridge
across a narrow creek.

My still camera is useless for him

We climb a long bank into a grove of trees.
Bird song in the lush green—
he whispers to his father, who lifts him
onto his shoulders, his head
just grazing the leaves.

(4/27/2003)

Life As a Real Dream

I wake in the middle of the night
feel my breath rushing itself.
I lay my hands across my chest
to steady it, but no—
it won't lay back. I am awake
and so rise softly to urinate,
tribute to a prostate gone to radiation.

I gather a blanket on the couch
and soon pass again to sleep—
awakened by my own name
spread across the dark.
Who calls me? A male voice
drawn out—I look around—
it is myself calling in a dream.

Once on a train out West
I heard a whistle in the night,
waited till I saw it was
from the train I was on.

I fill a glass at the sink.
A winter moonlight lies golden
on a freshly fallen snow
connecting all I see.
I hear clocks ticking;
my old dog rises finally
to be let out. He tramps
softly across the white.
I stand at the door
as cold bites my skin.
This waking is
another form of sleep.

Waking to Myself

My old glasses on the floor
before the fireplace, where I slept
through the sound of crickets melting
into a soft gurgling of stream
into a deep hum of night.

The dog sighs at my side
and does not rise as morning light
filters through curtains onto floor boards.
Across the ceiling, a story of wood
which I slowly read.

In a little while I will rise
wash the cups from last night
start the fire for coffee
and the others still sleeping.

But for now I lie still
touch the ashes of incense
from a clay dish to my lips.

(11/30/02)

Driving Up the Ohio River on Route 2 in Late Fall

Trees breathe colors in afternoon light
turning the river into a slate of sky.
My wife and I drive a West Virginia two laner
beside the long waters, by an old railroad track.

Fields of alfalfa bordered in brush turn golden brown
as we pass again old faces of houses,
the dark brick and windows of abandoned factories
that lead into quiet towns a few blocks long.

Two old men talk on a street corner,
point to the ground, the sky;
a woman carries her baby and grocery bag
to a blue pick-up truck as evening comes on.

Life flows on like a river apart
from the roadways and bridges.
A sign in a beauty shop reads, "Come on in,"
and we wish we could enter more deeply here.

But we have those slow miles before sleep.
Our car drinks them in passing.
So little we really know, so much we share—
driving up river, heading home.

(11/09/02)

Falling and Rising

Twice I saw my father fall
as if from sky to earth.

Once at the construction site
he stepped through sheeting
above a window space
landed upon one knee
gouged by cinder block.
I held the shovel and my breath
till he got up. *I'm okay,*
he signed with thumb and hand,
but I was not—*My father*
held there in my chest—
that hardest day of work.

The second was in the yard
adults playing volleyball
shouting as we looped it
or slammed it hard.
The yard was tilted so that
he came tumbling towards us
a man of sixty rolling hard.
He got up breathless
as we gathered around,
then laughed it off, his eyes
more hurt than pained.

Each time I watched it, felt him
falling down and through me
as he would one final time.

Seven: Our Intentions, Waking to It

Someone Somewhere

is writing a poem
right now as we sit here listening
breathing this moment. And somewhere
someone is touching another
as they sit in the dark of a car
held to the moment of their kissingness.
A porch light goes on and they laugh,
right now.

And somewhere
someone is giving birth in the light
taking the pain into the body
and giving back love in the little room.
Right now—Right now.

Someone somewhere is riding a bike
home in the twilight singing a new song
And someone is combing their hair in the street
waiting for a ride
and recalling a dream.

And somewhere
someone is cutting bread with a knife
handing it a slice at a time
into their hands.
Right now someone is turning eggs in a pan.
And someone is wiping a dish with a cloth
holding it clean in kitchen light
stacking it there on the shelf.

And somewhere
someone is telling a story
into the eyes of a child and believing it more.
And someone downstairs is ironing clothes
folding them and smelling
the warm breath of cotton.

And somewhere

someone is turning the earth
with a spade given to them
by their father and remembering
the things that he said.

And someone is lying in the fresh grass
staring up through the tree at the sky
forgetting anything but the night.
And someone is counting stars
pointing with the finger of a child at the moon.
And right now someone is promising love,
promising life forever. Right now.

Someone somewhere is falling asleep in a chair
while the news reports what they *think* we should know:

how some mother's son has taken a gun
and fired it into the face of some mother's son,
how some children have drowned or set fire to a house,
how battles rage in parts of the world
and suffering burns in the streets. We know.
We know!

Yet we also know and can never forget
that right now someone is holding another
taking them in their arms
kissing their hair and eyes, saying
"We love you...Come home...Rest here...
You've done wonderful things."

Right now someone somewhere is strumming a guitar
and waiting for the words
to sing us all into song.
And right now someone
is writing—reading—hearing—
moving a poem
into being.

Right here, right now.

Summer Visit

For Bob

Toward the end of summer
when all the grass is brown,
a rain will come.

My friend has driven up
from Columbus
to play guitar and spend the night.
We sit outside in lake wind
and talk of family and jobs,
of houses and dogs.

The branches of the maple
sway like dancing arms.

He tells me how he tries to be home
when his daughter comes from school;
I talk with mine on long college drives.
His son wants to move out; mine to get married.
Last time we spoke of the mystery of hair
grown upon their male legs.

Birds flit through trees;
the dog barks to join us.

At fifty, our fathers gone,
we each hold the rudder
through seas strange and dark.
"Some days at work," he sighs,
"I feel almost overwhelmed."
Born a week apart, we have always
spoken for each other.

The magnolia tree
shades our afternoon beers
as a cat walks through the yard.

I tell him how lonely it seems

without parents, and he nods.
"If it weren't for Ann," I say,

"it would be impossible."
"I know," he smiles across the afternoon.

Above the house comes the soft hoot
of mourning doves predicting rain.

He takes his guitar in hand
and walks us down an old blues tune.
We both lean forward into it knowing
the melody of pain. Soon evening will come
and we will go inside to eat.
For now his music is enough
for anyone who hears.

Listening to Tich Nyat Hanh on the Road to Detroit

You know this guy is alright
by the way he laughs at himself,
telling stories, talking sense, ringing chimes,
while the Michigan traffic zooms by me.
I have left my wife to go to a conference,
but I know she understands
my old need to carry a message.

The sun spreads a golden fire
across the deep fields of corn
as Tich begins to speak of love
"With love you must have understanding.
Without understanding love is painful."
And I stop the tape a moment
as those words touch my life.
"Without understanding love is painful."
It turns inside me…the pain
we all cause each other. The secret
to our being with joy or not.
Though my father never said he loved me,
he always understood me. I feel his love
now as the wheels roll over asphalt—
It was there in his eyes—in his needing to help.
So it is with my daughters and son.
We give the understanding that
only love can bring. Tich
comes back on to say, "When we give
this lovingkindness, it is we
who feel it first. It comes back to us."
And though I want to drive home to hold them all,
I drive on through late afternoon

listening and breathing as the landscape
moves through me like a light.

(10/13/2000)

Saying Farewell

for Bear

My dog died Tuesday, put to sleep
in his Vet's office, his head nestled
in my hands as he sunk then faded
erasing that line for both of us.

I hear dogs bark at night now and,
like Camus, think they are mine.
I look for him still in the shadows,
go to his bowl which isn't there.

I buried his warm body in the woods
out where we used to walk.
He's in a hundred poems of mine,
silent, waiting, or pulling on his leash.

I stroke my pillow, hold my grandson,
read to myself on the porch
where we sat in fading light.
I talk to the space he's left behind.

Autumn Visit

September 19, 2004

We stand at the grave of my dog among trees
and brushwood—my grandson, his mother, and I,
having left a Sunday dinner to place
a stone with his name on this ground.

Adam looks around at the wild underbrush and
up at us to ask *where*, then sets it down himself
by the small boulder I had rolled over the earth.
It's a simple ceremony among first autumn leaves
hanging loose above us like a funeral tent.
No one speaks as we survey the ground
yet I miss his short-legged closeness
his soft breathing beside my bed.

"Now you know where he is," I say
but know already he has gone
unleashed from his body, beyond the edge of field
into a light that falls everywhere upon us.

Sitting on the Porch of a Friend's Cabin Along Chapel Creek
for Mary Sue

The shallow stream glides by
under lush trees, bent as if to drink.
Soft sounds of bird songs, evening breeze
after a hot day. While others walk,
we sit in shade remembering
last time with our friend here
now gone beyond cancer.

Once we drummed along these banks
burning sage and candles into night
for her spirit and ours. Now we sit
in wordless quiet
feeling her again.

I look up to the evening sky
as a pair of rough-winged swallows
hurry by as if they are lost,
their soft underbellies aglow.
The stream glides homeward,
moving slowly, knowing the way.

Walking the Labyrinth in Early Fall

My wife and I set our morning coffee cups aside
on the back porch and drive out
to the local arboretum.

Ours is the second car in the parking lot—
sweet smell of asphalt and ragweed.
a light wind sends ripples across the pond
deep waves through grains of long grasses
thin and light as auburn hair.

We pause inside the arbor of wisteria
whose fragrance remind us
of close times with our lost friend.
The stone labyrinth is her memorial—
made from sandstone slabs her husband
hauled from a nearby quarry.
Her women friends chose a right design
to marry body and mind.

We enter the clearing near the trees
knowing all this, yet wanting to forget
and to just sink into the tall grasses.

My wife begins, then I in silence,
this timeless circling.
A robin calls, a cardinal,
a distant stream, the wind through trees,
early pulse of cicada—
the land comes inside us.
No thoughts, just a gentle centering
stepping through each moment, each wind-swept stone.
Slowly our life becomes what it is.

The Aftermath

I will not write the poem
of the War on America.
I will not speak the pain
we all have taken in
a hundred times
feeling the dark planes
crash through 10,000,000 lives,
severing reason from the brain.
Others will write those poems, I am sure.

Watching the faces of the young,
I pray for a brave wisdom.

For if intention can so disrupt
it can also re-connect.
And so I write of the wounded faces
filled with care, the tired hands
reaching others, pulling them
to safety there, of those
who bravely wait in rain.

I would write instead the poem
of sweet intention
inside my grandson's eyes
reading wild geese
across the skies,
my own wife turning
to hold me close,
my saying, "We'll get through this"
one more time and believing it
as I do the rain.

(9/18/2001)

Where You Are

My granddaughter fishes in the lake
with a plastic fish on her line.
Her practice is the real thing.

She, her mother, and baby brother
run over water on a sand bar—
Dancer and dance made one.

The baby has Buddha in his mouth,
a rubber one from a quarter machine.
If you meet the Buddha, eat him.

The Turnings

I think of spring again
as fall turns into winter.

Tadpoles swimming in my heart
flowers blooming in deep light
morning call of cardinal

I close my eyes to see again,
then rise and go out to birdfeeder
sparrows hungry in the trees;
bright leaves deepen red to brown,
become a quiet path
inside the sound of wind…
feathers on the ground.

Drumming

For Dave and Guilda

We gather chairs into a circle
dim the lights to just a candle
and begin patting the skins
tapping out a call for help
an expression of our world and self:
Drums along the Mohawk—Nigeria—Ecuador—
Blood measure of human tribe
played across the rivers into trees,
soft measure of birds echoing back
restoring each and all, balancing.
We go on through years.

Tasting the Day

I sit in my car sipping Chai tea
bought from the coffee shop
near the Jackson Street Pier.
Cold wind is pushing choppy waves
against the docks where the seagulls are
folded close to the snow-covered walk.

Like all of my friends
I have been worrying my life along,
not writing much of anything.
In an hour I will go to court
deciding a woman's fate
for the next thirty days.

The clouds are barely moving
and the tea is sweet.
And cold as it is, the sun is shining.
These gulls don't question anything.
The wind rustles their gray feathers
and rolls off their backs.

Reconciliation

A dog barks in a yard waking us.

Night snow has fallen all around;
the wind's voice across the land.
The newspaper rests in the yard.

As night comes on in shadows,
so it recedes into morning light,
soft sun rising slowly through the trees,
squirrel tracks in the snow.

We walk out into the cold
breathing it inside ourselves,
breathing ourselves out to it.
Starlings at a feeder spreading seeds.

We live in a field of energy
intimate and deep, bright mystery
of what is known unspoken.
Our footprints a map in snow.

(1/3/2005)

The Poetry Readings

Sitting at the table near the microphone
I eat a muffin with a friend.
We sip dark coffee and watch as local poets
rise to share themselves in the room.
I am so close I see their hands tremble
on sheets of words composed this week,
hear them breathe with deep intent,
sigh with sweet acceptance and applause.

I have been here before, joined the group
who witness and rage, sow love and laughter
like seeds cast upon an earthen floor.
And it is this that moves me now
in this pageant of bodies and voices
as each risk all to share—
words that speak for eyes and heart.

One man rises to drum his poem
tapping a wordless message out and through us.
I lean back and drink it in, then open eyes to see
how each has held an ear to earth
then risen to echo back
a felt transcription of what is there.

Beneath the words the same intention:
"This is how it feels to be alive."

Following the Road

I have left my wife at the airport,
flying out to help our daughter
whose baby will not eat.
And I am driving on to Kent
to hear some poets read tonight.

I don't know what to do with myself
when she leaves me like this.
An old friend has decided to
end our friendship. Another
is breaking it off with his wife.

I don't know what to say
to any of this—*Life's hard.*
And I say it aloud to myself,
Living is hard, and drive further
into the darkness, my headlights
only going so far.

I sense my own tense breath, this fear
we call stress, making it something else,
hiding from all that is real.

As I glide past Twin Lakes,
flat bodies of water under stars,
I hold the wheel gently, slowing my
body to the road, and know again that
this is just living, not a trauma
nor dying, but a lingering pain
reminding us that we are alive.

Waking to It

I wake early, step outside into snow,
bring in the news and begin to read
while coffee brews. The paper
is full of fear and threats
as governments prepare
to start another war. But what I feel
lies beyond the politics of power
to a sickness in the heart
an impotence to will a better way.

And then my grandson appears
down the stairs in my wife's arms,
and I forget all in his smiling face.
We drink coffee as he sips juice
eat warm oatmeal with honey and cream.
And as I watch him
lift each spoonful to his lips
I feel myself break—
Who could ask anyone
to kill another, to kill or be killed
take the wounds of war into
his body and mind?
An outrage to ask—America,
what have you become?
And yet I watch as
young are shipped out to foreign soil
where other young children
sit with their families
and lift these same spoons,

look up to the blue skies
in a world made unforgivable
by fear and lies.

My tears are all inside.

Celebrating Lao Tzu's Birthday at the Taoist Healing Center in Cleveland, Ohio

Funny how the traffic slows before the center
as if a river were seeking to eddy here.
We park along a warehouse and walk,
three guys out on a Monday evening—
laundry, coffeeshop, hairdresser, Taoist Healing Center.
We go inside where a small crowd of strangers
smile in silence, as Tao and wife Mei
gather food from the back—deep tubs of
fried rice, chop suey, and lo mein noodles,
aromas blending with sounds of a Chinese flute.

At the front a small altar holds plates of
apples, melons, bananas, a brass bucket of sand.
Behind it a painting of Lao Tzu.
To the side a cooler of pop, a table
with green tea in Styrofoam cups.
We sit in chairs and watch, hear the rush
of city noise each time someone enters.

Tao is instructing his son Ingold
on when to ring the chimes. Little Amy
is waiting for her words.
Mei turns the lights up, Tao turns them down.
She is dressed in slacks and blouse,
he in a saffron robe, black monk's cap.
In this little room there is no place
to hide their concern or joy.

Twenty or more persons await a sign,
when suddenly Tao announces:
"Okay. Welcome. We will do a blessing."
The father bows before the feet of Lao Tzu,
the son rings the chimes, each time
clearer than the last.
The daughter taps a wooden fish,
the mother greets latecomers at the door.
Together in silence we bow three times before Lao,

then Tao rises and beckons us, "Now we eat."
We form a soft line to the food
all warm and spiced with a spirit
we have never tasted. An easy talk
fills the room, all of us humble and light.

Later we will each light an incense stick
and hear Tao's praise of Lao Tzu.
While a bus goes by someone reads:
>   Who knows
>   doesn't talk.
>   Who talks
>   doesn't know.
Then we all sit a long time entering the silence,
all of us knowing the *Tao Te Ching* will ring
in our lives for days like gentle wings
or the taste of our saliva,
like the touch of incense smoke upon our skin.

Mourning the Death of My Taoist Healer
After Chia Tao

My reflection in the windows
of your closed shop—
where will I go for health?

March snow in the stone fountain,
black birds deep in the bushes,
the silence of city streets at dawn.

Sitting in our favorite café
I watch the slow traffic of faces,
allow my coffee to grow cold.

A white pigeon
walks on a black car—
the snow has turned to rain.

From my coat pocket
a worn copy of the *Tao Te Ching*,
your voice in the pages.

I blame myself for these tears
a man who still misses
the emptiness of all things.

Brothers and Sisters

I kneel by our bay window
sanding the fresh white pine
while sparrows gather at the feeder
and on the snow covered ground.
Morning sun lights my work,
my arms burn with it.
I push, I watch, I feel
the roughness disappear,
the smoothness becoming real.

Last night I stood with others
in Ebenezer Baptist Church
for Martin Luther King, Jr.
An old woman in a flowered hat
took my hand and swayed to song.
Tentative at first, her grip
became more warm and firm.
We spoke as the words: "I love you...
You are important to me."
Each time the words becoming more true.

(1/17/2005)

Doing a Drop-In Visit the Day After Christmas

I have driven out early in the cold
to visit this other family,
a service to the courts.
I cross a yard of snow and starlings
and knock at their back door.

"I been expectin' you," he smiles
knowing the ruling that
binds us. He hands me a
cup of coffee while his kids
play at his feet. I say,
"I appreciate your letting me in."

The smallest child, my charge,
holds a naked Barbie by the hair,
offers me a handful of M&M's.
Her stepsister motions me in,
"Here, you can sit here."
Her brother grins, "I'm nine today.
I got a new Red Ryder BB gun."
(I smile back knowing I will not report this.)
Paul sits between us, says
"I won't allow him to shoot it in the house."
I nod and sip my coffee.

The house is warm, presents and paper
scattered under their small tree.
He has shaven today, is wearing
his new flannel shirt. They each
tell me of their Christmas gifts
begin to speak of their lives. I listen
to this family of another man
that slowly becomes my own.

Branches in a Stream

Bare trees in morning fog
live inside me.

Red leaves turning in wind
blow through me.

Sparrows feed on seeds
in our stone garden.

Bamboo chimes in wind
teeking and toking.

Young boy runs through yard
pulling my strength.

Old man of me
spreads crumbs on earth.

No distance out or in—
branches in a stream

breathing what is there.

The Laboring

I wrestle and moan over retirement plans,
long for it like a woman in red.
The sky feels heavy on my back,
the leaves I rake are made of stone.

My dog barks, runs after a squirrel
into the neighbor's yard.
I yell and curse at him,
curse myself for renting others
space in my mind and heart.

There are too many words
knocking together like leaves
still hanging to the trees.

I breathe the fall air
rake again and again
till all there is is work.

Retirement

37 years of teaching
stacked clean like lumber
to the splintery rafters,
and ten thousand faces
stretched across a sea.
Other tasks grow inside me
for the journey home.

Traveling Home

In retirement now
    I've come to know my life.
Standing outside my work clothes
    I feel naked on the porch.

When regrets come,
    I wander into the yard,
bring out the lawn mower,
    the trimmer, the planter.

I take my work in doses,
    watch birds gather at the feeder.
The sun comes up and goes down.
    Clouds pass overhead.

I leave my books
    sitting on the shelves,
take the old dog
    for a walk along the lake.

Bird song rises up
    above the rush of traffic.
The way leads back
    to where it begins.

(8/11/2003)

The Change

I've shaved off my mustache
gray hairs and shaving cream
dripping down into the sink—
thirty years.

In the shower I shampoo,
brush suds across a bare lip.

Mirror shock each morning—
my brother, my father, my shadow self
through all these years.

My son and daughter stare,
my grandson turns aside—
"You look...*different!*"
big word to capture it.

My wife delights at
having this younger man.

Friends question my face with their own,
but who am I to answer?

Like searching the house for—
glasses, wallet, keys—
I remember all that I've done,
then let it go to discover
where I am now.

(9/7/2003)

Satori Walking

Camera opens in extreme close-up
pans in slow motion
your room in morning light:
gray socks on carpet, sleeping dog,
keys on dresser top, empty glass—
facts as truths, truths as facts.
The world empty and close. Your room
becomes yourself, only skin and bones.

You rise to walk the hallway
Each step a breath, each breath a step.
Outside a dog barks, a car rolls by,
wind blowing through trees. Inside a
breath opens and closes
stepping through shadows and light.

As a child I lay on porch steps,
watched ants between bricks, sunlight
turning their red bodies to gold. And I
closed my eyes, emptied thought…
let go to nothing…the here and now.
Camera fades to white.

Sleeping with the Remote

for Ann

I find it lying between us now
thin plastic case beside my leg
near the warmth of your soft skin.

The last thing I saw last night
was your hair, your sleeping face
in the light.
                    A thousand, thousand
days and nights, as lovers and friends,
husband and wife.
                                Sometimes
we dance and sing, sometimes we watch
and laugh together. Then I
push the power button off
move next to your soft shore
guided by your sweet breath
where nothing is remote.

Secret Sharer

She sleeps beside me in the car as I drive into
   the wind and her face is more familiar
than the fields, so close to my own that I reach
   over and stroke her hair without waking
anything more than my love for her
   breathing softly as wind through river willows
And I stare ahead counting the cows
   guiding us homeward through the miles.

Just Sweeping

A man sweeps his garden path
of twigs and leaves and stones.
With a tug he discovers
the small body of a squirrel,
its smooth, brown shaded fur.

For a moment he looks up
into the trees—then
places it on the rock garden
where it can meet the sun and rain,
perhaps an eagle's sight.

Bellingham Breakfast

Sitting in the Old Town Café
we wait for our eggs,
as a few white clouds
float over Lummi Island.

My granddaughter plays
with her sausage.
My wife and daughter
sip tea.
        My head
is full of worries
as we talk of world concerns,
how much to be involved...?

And I am feeling almost overwhelmed
    when I look down
        at the sunlit skin
            on the wrist of our waitress
    pouring coffee
into my cup.
                (5/30/2005)

Our Touch

She sits by his bedside into late afternoon,
watches sunlight fill and empty his glass,
breathes in the pain of their room,
his hands cool yet smooth on the sheets,
breathes out a peace and love.
His face holds their history together
and she strokes it, the coolness of his hair,
as evening spreads across the room

It comes down to this,
no more, no less:
We live by our intentions
the way we give ourselves,
not what we hold but how.
Our breath teaches this…
gentle karma of energy flow.

The hawk gliding on wind
willow branches bending low;
the waters flow over rocks;
bright leaves turn and fall.

She reaches to wipe his brow;
a child's hand taking yours.

The music sings within,
our self in our hands
our being in our touch
we live by letting go.

Without Wind

Tonight I want to sit on the porch
as the darkness comes through the trees
and hear the last birds of evening
while my coffee cools in my cup.
In a while I will rise and go in
to sit in the room with my wife.
But for now I want to sit alone
my hands folded on my lap,
my breath one with the night.

The Bonds of Work

"We'll get the job done,"
I tell my daughter on the phone
and hear my father's voice, all his life
turning work to love and honor.
"We'll get the job done"—not perfection
but carry through, and I recall
the long hours of getting his tools
holding flashlights while he lay
on cardboard beneath the car
fixing brakes and starters, changing oil
because he could, because we
needed milk and bread.

When married, he'd help us move
each time not stopping till the beds
were up in each bedroom—his hands
red from lifting, turning wrenches
on appliances, thinking his way through.
And he'd follow our U-Haul back,
return with me and sandwiches,
my wife making the kids' beds,
Mom serving coffee in paper cups,
only then could we sit and rest.

I give back now this work
for my children grown and wed,
helping them know their grandfather's
love by the work he bred.

Sunday Service in the Ohio Valley

I stand in cemetery snow
one foot on each grave:
my father—my mother, to ask
forgiveness, announce great grandchildren
they would love and somehow
already know.

I drive to their old church,
enter silent and penitent
greeted by smiling children and
the chubby hands of old members.
The church attendance is as sparse
as a winter garden, so I sing stronger
to keep the tunes alive. Up the aisle
comes my aging aunt in the choir,
nodding to me and to life.

> Yesterday I stood at the edge of town
> looking down at the abandoned stadium
> a ruined school bus in a field of snow,
> the lights of the mill without sound,
> freight cars dead on their tracks.
> Wearing a coat of loss I turned,
> walked back into town, and stood a long time
> watching the Catholic school children
> gliding over new snow tracks.
> Breathing in and out I gave up forever
> trying to move the past into the present.
> And I said to myself again and again:
> "What was—was, / and what is—is,"
> my eyes and heart bound in this
> comfort chorus of a visit home
> "What was—was, / and what is—is"
> This old truth there in the earth and air

At the church recessional, I wake,
the words flowing from my lips:

"Let there be peace on earth,
And let it begin with me."

I close the door on my aunt's car,
and sparrows rise to snowy skies.

Larry Smith is a poet, fiction writer, critic, biographer, and editor. A native of the industrial Ohio River Valley in Mingo Junction, Ohio, he taught for three decades at Firelands College of Bowling Green State University in Huron, Ohio, where he has lived with his wife, Ann, and their three children, now adults and parents themselves. In 2004 he co-edited with poet Ray McNiece the Harmony anthology *America Zen: A Gathering of Poets*, and in 2005 he co-edited with wife Ann, the anthology *Family Matters: Poems of Our Families* (both from Bottom Dog Press). His biography, *Kenneth Patchen: Rebel Poet in America* appeared in 2000 from a Consortium of Small Presses. He is the director of The Firelands Writing Center and of Bottom Dog Press. This is his eighth book of poems following *Milldust and Roses: Memoirs* (Ridgeway Press 2001).